RECLAIMING
The
REFORMATION

CHRIST FOR YOU IN COMMUNITY

RECLAIMING
The
REFORMATION

CHRIST FOR YOU IN COMMUNITY

Magnus Persson

TRANSLATED BY **BROR ERICKSON**

Reclaiming the Reformation: Christ for You in Community

Published by:
1517 Publishing
PO Box 54032
Irvine, CA 92619–4032

Publisher's Cataloging-In-Publication Data
(Prepared by The Donohue Group, Inc.)

Names: Persson, Magnus, 1973- author. | Erickson, Bror, translator, editor.
Title: Reclaiming the Reformation : Christ for you in community / by Magnus
    Persson ; translated and edited by Bror Erickson.
Other Titles: Kristi kyrka. English
Description: Irvine, CA : 1517 Publishing, [2021] | Translation of: Kristi kyrka.
    [Uppsala] : EFS Budbäraren, [2017]. | Includes bibliographical references.
Identifiers: ISBN 9781948969710 (hardcover) | ISBN 9781948969727 (paperback) |
    ISBN 9781948969734 (ebook)
Subjects: LCSH: Church renewal. | Jesus Christ—Presence.
Classification: LCC BV600.3 .P47413 2021 (print) | LCC BV600.3 (ebook) | DDC
    262.0017—dc23

Printed in the United States of America

Cover art by Brenton Clarke Little

First and foremost, I dedicate this American edition and translation of my first book to my first grandchild Bjorn Aaron Meissner, born in 2018, who is a US citizen living in Minneapolis. On the same Sunday I was ordained into the priestly office, I had the joy of baptizing you in the name of the Father and the Son and the Holy Spirit. I pray that your generation will see a complete gospel reformation. I pray that you will rediscover and trust the comfort delivered in Word and Sacrament, reclaim the riches of the evangelical Reformation and so restore the church to radiate the glory of God revealed in Christ crucified for you, and reverberate it to the very ends of the earth.

I also dedicate this book to all my long-time friends in ministry around the globe. For many years I traveled the world and preached in your churches and conferences. I am richer because of the different experiences and acquaintances I have gained in these circles, whether Pentecostal, seeker-sensitive, charismatic, missional, or non-denominational. But Jesus said: "For what does it profit a man to win the whole world and lose his soul?" (Mark 8:36) This English translation allows you to follow my theological journey and dig into the core convictions regarding Christ's Church that drove my reorientation from relevant to reformational. I am eager to share it with you.

By God's grace for God's glory.

Magnus Persson
August the 16th, 2021

Contents

Prelude. Deformation or Reformation......................................ix

Chapter 1. Evangelical Catholicity.. 1
Chapter 2. Christianity's (Divinely Instituted) Means of Grace.........17
Chapter 3. Charismatic..31
Chapter 4. The Word..53
Chapter 5. Baptism..79
Chapter 6. The Lord's Supper... 97
Chapter 7. The Keys 115
Chapter 8. The Office 131
Chapter 9. Divine Service..151
Chapter 10. The Cross 175

Postlude. The Church I See 189
Notes... 195

Deformation
or Reformation

Concerning the Current Condition of the Church

. . . However the church is not only an association of external ties and rites like other civic organizations, but it is principally an association of faith and the Holy Spirit in the hearts of persons. It nevertheless has its external marks so that it can be recognized, namely, the pure teaching of the gospel and the administration of the sacraments in harmony with the gospel of Christ. Moreover, this church alone is called the body of Christ, which Christ renews, sanctifies, and governs by his Spirit as Paul testifies in Ephesians 1 [22–23], when he says, "And [God] has made him the head over all things for the church, which is his body, the fullness of him who fills all in all." [. . .] For the true unity of the church it is sufficient to agree on the teaching of the gospel and the administration of the sacraments. It is not necessary that everywhere human traditions or rites or ceremonies instituted by human beings be the same. [. . .] We did not have trivial reasons for presenting this article. For it is evident that many foolish opinions about traditions have crept into the church.[1]

The Marks of the Church

Many voices both inside and outside the church have spoken about the church's impending death. Yet, in writing this book, I would rather cry out loudly: Long live the church! What is it that actually guarantees that the church will continue to live? It is the Lord of the church himself, the resurrected Jesus Christ who lives and reigns in eternity. The same Spirit, who woke Christ from the dead, is still active today in his body, Christ's church. Yet many of us have various experiences concerning churches that are more dead than alive. The church's condition must be taken seriously and ought to lead us to soul searching and prayer. However, uneasiness over the church's condition is also fertile ground for all sorts of creative ideas concerning how the church should change and what we ought to do to guarantee her survival and growth. The spirit of the day rewards superficiality and effectiveness, so there are many who want to take a pragmatic approach that proceeds from what seems to work and attracts the masses. This way of thinking has taken the field in today's Christendom. The audience is to be enticed, and the message sold with attractive packaging and the promise of great and quick results. Christians take stock of contemporary trends, and they attempt to "listen to the market" to catch the winds of change. Yet, this approach and the fluctuations associated with it have left many exhausted and spiritually poor. We have become disillusioned and worn out. This book also risks being conceived of as yet another call for another sort of creative change. However, the motive behind this book is to steer past contemporary applicable trends and turn toward the timeless truth that has deep roots and offers a robust foundation and firm ground under our feet.

The question that this book deals with is this: *What is Christ's church?* A person could, of course, answer this question in many different ways. For example, a person could point to such things as basic Christian teaching, people who believe in God and celebrate the Divine Service regularly, the diaconate, mission work, evangelization, and so on. Yet a new path opens if we approach the question while considering what is central to the church and thus essential. So, perhaps we should reformulate the question and ask: what is central to the church and what are her most important marks? This is what I have summarized and wanted to discuss in this book, those things that are central to the church, her most important "marks" or characteristics. This will be the first book of a series called RE:FORM. In future books, I want to discuss each individual mark in more detail. The purpose of this series will be to draft the contours of a program for congregational reform and life that rests on the foundation of the Reformation.

Common Christian theology usually speaks about four signs (marks) of Christ's church. These are taken from the words of the Nicene Creed concerning the church as one, holy, catholic, and apostolic. These are also foundational for reformational and Protestant Christendom. Yet, in light of the decay in which the church found itself during the late Middle Ages, a discussion came about concerning specific marks. How could a person know where this one, holy, catholic,[2] and apostolic church is found? Martin Luther also dealt with this subject. In many of his writings, he labored with different lists of marks of the church whereby three were always emphasized: the Word, baptism, and the Lord's Supper. In all of Luther's discussions about the essence of the church, the Word is the first and most foundational. The gospel of Christ is the center around which everything else in his theology revolves. In the year 1539, Luther wrote the book "On Councils and the Church." The purpose of this book was to clear away everything that obscured Christ's church and, thus, the pure gospel. He wanted to formulate visible, conceptual signs rooted in the Bible to help common people distinguish the true essence of the church against the background of diverse abuses and aberrations. In that book, he pointed out the *seven marks* that will be considered in this book series.

Characteristic features are important when a person looks for something, for example, a person or a thing. If a person does not know what he is seeking, its attribute or marks, neither does he know how to look for it, nor will he be able to determine if he has found the right one. When something has disappeared, a description of the different attributes that delineate that which is lacking becomes necessary for a person to begin his search for what is missing. So how does a person identify *Christ's church*? Or to use theological jargon: What are the marks by which Christ's church is constituted? Are there objective signs in Christ's church that are applicable in all times and cultures and which therefore make it possible to identify her? By asking questions of this type, Luther discerned different marks of the true church. His heart was beating for simple Christians who sought to differentiate between true Christianity and a false and broken Christendom where many, and often contradictory, conceptions made themselves applicable. In Luther's own words: "But how will or how can a poor confused person tell where such Christian holy people are to be found in this world?"[3]

Luther presented the following seven marks as those that constitute and characterize the church where Christ is present and active: the *Word*, *Baptism*, the *Lord's Supper*, the *Keys*, the *Office*, the *Divine Service* (*worship*) and the *Cross*. These are neither new nor peculiar things; rather, they are very foundational if a person starts with the Bible and then proceeds to the universal Christian tradition. Reformation is needed when and where these marks are missing because reformation concerns itself with reestablishing these foundational marks. Wherever one or more of these seven marks have been diverted, distorted, or obscured by diverse human inventions and additions, reformation is needed. So, these signifying marks are concerned with what is absolutely foundational for the Christian church and central to her calling: the gospel of Jesus Christ, his death and resurrection for the sake of our salvation, and how this gospel and salvation are mediated to us through the church. These marks shift the focus from external forms and structures to the very essence. They do not occupy us with theological hairsplitting and external distinctions, but they direct us to the very core around which the church is gathered and established. Without these marks, the church is like a ghost, or a body without a soul, a piece of meat with no structure or purpose. Everything concerns itself with Jesus Christ, where he allows himself to be found, and through which means he has promised to be present for the purpose of giving us his good gifts. So, the search for the marks of the church is not a search for a pure and unblemished church without sin, weakness, and challenges—if anyone thought that such a church existed. Rather, it is a search for the place where sinners can find a gracious God, the God who reveals himself in the gospel. As the Swedish theologian Folke T. Olofsson said so wonderfully:

> The church consists of a disorderly and noisy building site with "Christians under construction." In the church there are great

sinners who stagger forth from one absolution after the other, and great saints, who though they shine for others, despair of their own salvation . . . This therefore is a reason to repeat that the church's holiness is not the sum of her members. Holiness grows under the shadow of the holiness that Christ gives the church. The church has a share in Christ's righteousness and because of him, she may consider it her own.[4]

I do not hide my influences in this book. Martin Luther is the chief influence, but there are also the influences of Carl Olof Rosenius and Bo Giertz. These servants of the Lord have been instrumental in my personal journey as they have opened wide the treasure chambers of both the Scriptures and the history of the church. In various ways, they have helped me to see Christ and all his benefits more clearly, the good news of the gospel more distinctly, and the true essence of Christ's church more fully. In Luther, I have come into contact not only with the theology of the Reformation, but also the heritage of the whole church: a genuinely catholic Christianity. Rosenius helped me to rightly divide law and gospel, to see the gospel in all its glory and how it answers the deepest existential dilemma of man. Giertz's vision of Christ's church has in great part been a blueprint for how I myself think about the congregational life of a reformational church and how I express that in this book.[5] Neither am I ashamed to acknowledge that, for the most part, the thoughts I present are neither new nor my own but have been imparted to me through the writings and books of these theologians and churchmen. I write from a common Christian vision and make use of common Christian language, but with a distinctively Lutheran dialect. However, it will not escape notice that I also have a charismatic and non-denominational accent. I am very thankful for the dedicated and vibrant spirituality, the earnest concern for evangelism, and bold faith in God with which the charismatic movement has enriched me. So, I hope to be able to express a warm and bold Pentecostal spirituality that is deeply rooted in a solid reformation theology, formed and expressed by a common catholic liturgy and missional ecclesiology.

The De-formation of the Church and the Need for Re-formation

When I emphasize the church's need for reformation in this book, I'm not pointing at any particular context. When the Reformation occurred during the late Middle Ages, the point was obviously directed against the Roman Catholic Church, but today the message of the Reformation is directed to the same degree at Protestant ranks; this is a message that the whole evangelical church family needs to hear together. This means historical church bodies, evangelical denominations, as well as non-denominational networks. To you Lutherans in particular—high church as well as low church—I write as a former pastor of a modern Pentecostal church who has discovered the riches that belong to you but seem to be way too often neglected by you. Some of you even seem ashamed of your reformational heritage and desperately seek other paths for renewal of the church rather than those of the Reformation. I write to my brothers and sisters in the evangelical, charismatic, and non-denominational camps, as one coming from their own ranks, yet as one who has made a pilgrimage *ad fontes* through the bountiful history and traditions of theology and ecclesiology and discovered irreplaceable riches that our churches may take advantage of. So, the church's reformation is not about fragmentation, but a way forward to unity around that which is central to the church, around Christ and him crucified. So, to be protestant, even if I personally do not like the term, does not primarily mean to protest against something but to be *pro*, thus, for something. The Reformation's chief glory is nothing but the gospel, that wonderful message concerning undeserved grace that flows out from the cross of Christ. To reform the church means that this joyous message should always stand in the center of the church and shape her worship, message, and mission. Simply put, it means putting the *evangel* back into the evangelical church, reclaiming the common Christian (apostolic and catholic) ground, a return to and a reestablishment of evangelical catholicity. However, to restore the church's center in the spirit of the Reformation means, now as it did then, that a person must ask certain critical questions, point out abuses and failures, and call people to repentance, back to Christ. Therefore, the first step to personal and congregational reformation is to recognize the deformation of the church that has occurred and continues to occur because of the reality of sin.

We live in a fallen world where everything expires. Our bodies and minds decay, hearing decreases, and vision weakens. We all find ourselves on a downhill slope and are constantly surrounded by destructive forces. Spiritual decay has been a recurring element among God's people since the days of the Old Covenant and throughout the whole history of the church. God's people stray from faith, and the central truths that were formerly held in high regard are obscured, distorted, and, finally, denied. We are all sinners with an inherent distortion that constantly lures us the wrong way. We are like cars with skewed alignments that veer toward the ditch or oncoming traffic if the driver does not have a firm grip on the wheel. This is what we call original or inherited sin. All of us from birth are deformed by a deep mistrust of God's goodness and are drawn to that which opposes God. Sin's deepest meaning is that men have lost their trust in God and have tried to commandeer the driver's seat because they fear that life will not be as good as it could be if they do not take control themselves. So, the innermost essence of sin does not deal with immorality even if such things are always the consequence of a loss of trust in God.

This inherited sin remains with us even after we have come to faith in Christ, and it is something we must battle for the rest of our lives. In the words of Luther, this righteousness that God bestows upon us and that the gospel proclaims to us is an "alien righteousness" (*iustitia aliena*), namely, Christ's own righteousness. It does not consist of an actual or inner righteousness that replaces our sinful nature, but it comes to us from another One. So, it comes to us as a gift that is completely independent of us, from the outside. When we are justified, or declared righteous by grace through faith, it is not because of anything we have achieved through our good works or personal piety, but because of something done for us and imputed to us. Sin is not counted against us when we live by faith in Christ, but our ingrained distrust of God will remain until the day of resurrection. Sin causes us to be curved in on ourselves. Among other things, this shows itself in the inclination to trust more in our own reason than God's promise. Priests, pastors, and church leaders do not escape this sinful reality either. The fear of failure, the striving after the recognition of men, and the desire for success in ministry gives a lot of fuel to our inherent affections. Do we, even in the midst of our work for the church, dare trust that God's Word is sufficient and powerful to carry out God's work in our time? Do we trust that Christ is present as he has promised through the means he has instituted? This is an important question that we constantly need to ask ourselves.

Just as it is with us individual believers, the church as a whole does not need to do anything in particular to be deformed. Just being in and living in this world means that we are put under the pressure and influence of the spiritual powers of the day. The different powers that are active in our contemporary setting strive to form us according to this world and its mentality. Perhaps today we are bombarded more than at any other time by different messages that arouse our desires, shape our ambitions, and guide our thoughts. The church may exist, if it only adapts itself according to the ruling norms and doesn't make any claim that can be conceived of as alien or offensive. The problem is that the spirit of the day speaks so clearly in the language of our hearts, because our hearts are deformed by the power of sin. For this reason, the Christian life cannot proceed from the often-heard cliché that a man should "listen to his heart"—it is precisely the heart that is the problem (Matt 15:19)! The deformation is ongoing, so reformation is constantly needed, a return to the center and core of the faith. Martin Luther saw this clearly. His first thesis of the 95 that he nailed to the door of the church in Wittenberg 500 years ago was: "When our Lord and Master Jesus Christ said, 'Repent' (Matt. 4:17), he willed the entire life of believers to be one of repentance."[6]

The True Glory of the Reformation

The five-hundredth anniversary of the Reformation took place in 2017, with great celebratory events here in Sweden in the Lund Cathedral and in the Malmö Arena, with the Bishop of Rome (Pope Francis) in attendance. Ecumenism and unity stood in the center of praiseworthy initiatives by the Lutheran World Federation and the Vatican. There is good reason for all church families and traditions to take note of this and study the texts that are gathered in the document *From Conflict to Communion.*[7] But is it really possible to unite around unity? Or is real unity a fruit of the Spirit's work through the gospel? When the praiseworthy ecumenical ambitions are set in motion, the question arises around what center we shall gather and be united. The question is as decisive for local congregations as it is for national and global ecumenicism. The naïve and simple answer is, of course, Jesus! What, other than Jesus, would we gather around as a Christian church? But many voices and movements claim the name of Jesus, and at the deepest level there are many different understandings of what the gospel really is about. And it is precisely right there that the Reformation has something to say to the church concerning her current affairs. The Reformation dealt with the determination of that which was central and indispensable—to locate the center around which all ecclesiological life and theological quests revolve—so that we can constantly rediscover and return to this center.

Here there is reason to name the Ecumenical Creeds or *Symbola* (Latin for mark) that have been foundational since the days of the early church: The Apostles Creed, the Nicene Creed, and the Athanasian Creed. With a brilliant mix of simple yet ample conclusions of the central themes, they sketch the dogmas around which this Christian faith revolves. In the Nicene Creed, we confess our faith in the "one holy, catholic, and apostolic church." This is crucial. But how will it come into manifestation? How does a person recognize this one, holy, catholic, and apostolic church? The Augsburg Confession, the basis for the vast majority of Lutheran churches in the world, is the first confessional document to give a fuller picture:

> Likewise they teach that one holy church will remain forever. The church is the assembly of saints in which the gospel is taught purely and the sacraments are administered rightly. And it is enough for the true unity of the church to agree concerning the teaching of the gospel and the administration of the sacraments. It is not necessary that human traditions, rites or ceremonies instituted by human beings be alike everywhere.[8]

Despite the many centuries in which the *Confessio Augustana* (with its Apology), as it is called in Latin, has been the central document for the Lutheran Church, it is relatively unknown or just overlooked in our day. In this book series, I often reference this confession for many reasons. It is a confession with clear ecumenical claims. Its contents are fully evangelical and completely catholic. It outlines the doctrinal groundwork for what we can call the reformational church and the reformational gospel. Naturally, it marries well with the seven marks that Luther describes, the seven marks that provide the framework for this book series. I hope to be able to stir up some life and interest in this confession with these books. I want to remind those who already acknowledge the Confessio Augustana of what it has to say to us today, and make it known to those who are not yet very familiar with it. I believe that this confession can offer a solid and common ground and a path to renewal and rediscovery of Christ's church.

In today's Christendom, the external forms of the church's expression and activity are often discussed by pastors and church leaders. Most often, this discussion revolves around the question of what the church should do and how it should position itself to reach out and be attractive. The message is most often "do this" rather than "believe this." Rather than returning to its central message, means, and mission, the church often tries to find something new that meets the demands of the marketplace. As a rule, these endeavors put what is central on the back burner and make it obscure with different strategies and methods. Congregations become more occupied by the format and container than the content. So, there is reason to focus on what it is that carries the church's central content and commission to the world. Good intentions and pious hopes do not make any group a church. Neither does referencing the Bible every now and again or speaking about Jesus in general terms create a congregation of the people of God. So we return to the questions that introduced this chapter: what are the marks of Christ's church? What is it that makes a group of people into the body of Christ, in and through which Christ speaks and works in the world? What does one gather around and how is it expressed and manifested? Who can make the claim to be Christ's church? How does an individual recognize such a church and such a Christian people? Luther's seven marks can serve as an instrument for both reformation and unity as we answer these questions. So, I will examine these marks and present them throughout the rest of this book, after the three introductory chapters, to show how they can guide the church even today.

CHAPTER 1

Evangelical Catholicity

Concerning the Church's Common Identity

Nathan Söderblom[1] sometimes used the expression "evangelical catholicity." It sounds Roman Catholic, yet he did not understand it this way. In fact, this expression is found already in the foremost representative of Lutheran Orthodoxy, Johann Gerhard.[2] Something that Söderblom was quite conscious of. [. . .] Söderblom saw a program for the future, for the achievement of the church's unity in diversity. The gospel guarantees unity as a spiritual unity that we confess in our faith. Differences that exist in different traditions do not need to jeopardize unity. They can in fact enrich it because they mirror the diversity of God's revelation. God encounters man in different cultural and national milieus. So every church's peculiarity should be taken seriously.[3]

We Believe in a Universal Church

We confess our faith in a universal church with the Nicene Creed, which is heard every Sunday in churches of various traditions all over the world. As always, faith deals with something we cannot see with the naked eye but is assured by God's Word. What is it we confess when we use the expression "universal church"? The original word is "catholic." This word is used to describe the church in all three ecumenical creeds. But the word is older than the creeds. This word is already found in the letters of St. Ignatius of Antioch, a second-century apostolic father. Thus, it is in the generation directly succeeding the apostles that Ignatius writes: "Just as where Jesus Christ is, there is the Catholic Church..."[4] The Greek word *katholikós* has two root words, *kata*, which means of/with, and *holos* which means wholeness/fullness. In our day the word catholic is often equated with Roman Catholic. When I use the word, I am not referring to any specific church tradition, but to the whole of the Christian church's inheritance, message, and function throughout history. Christ's church has always been catholic to her core. The best description of the church's catholicity is that it is enveloped in and carried by the fullness of Christ. Paul expresses this truth with staggering descriptions like, "and gave him as head over all things to the church, which is his body, the fullness of him who fills all in all" (Eph. 1:22–23) and, "For in him the whole fullness of deity dwells bodily, and you have been filled in him, who is the head . . ." (Col. 2:9–10). So our confession of the church's catholicity is nothing less than a confession of the fullness of Christ as it has come to be expressed by Christ's church throughout the whole of history. We do not simply confess to certain parts or fragments of the church, not only that which is typical of our own Christian tradition. Christ's church is greater and wider than our local context or our specific community of faith. The roots of the church stretch further back than, for example, the arrival of the Pentecostal movement in 1906 or the beginning of the Reformation in 1517. Yes, in fact, even further back than the time of the Apostles. "All things are yours," as Paul writes (1 Cor. 3:21). The fourth-century church father Cyril of Jerusalem summarized the contents of the church's catholic nature in the following way:

> The church is called catholic because she is spread out over the whole world, to every corner of the earth, and because she unceasingly proclaims all doctrines that people need to know. Because she nurtures all kinds of people into a right fear of God, be they in powerful positions or ordinary citizens, be they learned or uneducated; because she has healing and remedy for all kinds of sins, soul and body; and because she possesses all kinds of virtues in deeds and in words as well as all kinds of spiritual gifts.[5]

This Christian church does not start from the beginning in every new generation, but it builds upon the same foundation with the same contents and within the same framework that has been given since its beginning. As a physical body, the church is constantly renewed but still remains the same body with the same soul. She carries her experiences, memories, and insights from times past with her. A true stewardship of this rich inheritance prepares the church to meet new times and challenges. Our physical bodies can be wounded and injured, but these injuries do not cause us to reject or abandon our bodies nor to try and create new ones. When the body suffers, is abused or disfigured, we seek healing and rehabilitation. It is in like manner with the church that is Christ's body. Christ watches over his body, over her every limb and part. His own body has encountered death and resurrection in glory to never die again, and he has given himself to the church. No one or nothing can extinguish the life of Christ's body because it is Christ's indestructible life that fills it. Individual local congregations can fall or be extinguished, but Christ's body remains in eternity.

The Church's Customs and Traditions

A body has certain orders and functions. Life does not just flutter about as an invisible substance. It is always found within the structured framework of a physical body. At the beginning of our Bibles, we read that God breathed his life spirit into Adam's body, and in a similar way God has breathed the life of the Holy Spirit into the body of Christ. The life of Christ pulsates in this body, and through this body, Christ is manifested in the world. Thus, the church is no abstract community but a visible and concrete assembly. Therefore, to hold fast to the church's particular framework, Christ's body, and the given contents of the faith does not mean that the spiritual life is stifled or that we are deprived of spiritual experiences and mysteries. On the contrary, it is actually this framework and given content of faith that is the prerequisite for spiritual life to flood in and be delivered according to God's will through God's instituted means. The imagined opposition between life and doctrine, freedom and order, that is so common in our day builds upon a false understanding of how God works. To speak of the church's established doctrine and order, to be confessional, is not particularly popular today. It is not considered "inspiring"; rather, it is regarded as authoritarian and limiting, or stale and lifeless. However, when, as happens in both success and adversity, pressure on the church and individual Christians intensifies, when inspiration fails us or confusion affects us, it is good to have something to hold to and lean on for support. The simple realization that it is not we who carry the church but the church that carries us comes as a relief.

These churchly orders and the content of the faith have a different name: tradition. The word comes from the Latin *tradere* and means "to hand over something." Where the Bible and the church are concerned, tradition deals with retelling and handing over tested and approved theology, patterns of sound teaching, formulations of the faith, liturgies, and customs of the divine service. So, tradition is rather important for the church because we otherwise would need to reinvent the wheel in every generation. A citation that is sometimes ascribed to Sir Thomas More and sometimes to the famous composer Gustav Mahler illuminates the meaning of tradition: "Tradition is not the worship of ashes, but the preservation of fire and the passing of the flame." Thus, tradition is not synonymous with traditionalism where a person mechanically and mindlessly repeats word and actions without any care or thought about what is being done. Someone has formulated it in the following way: "Tradition is the living faith of the dead. Traditionalism is the dead faith of the living." So, in this good sense, tradition is the living faith of our ancestors, something that needs to be handed over to new generations that, in their turn, need to learn to discover and appreciate the wealth they possess in the great inheritance of the church.

Tradition accommodates and carries the church, gives her patterns, actions, and symbols for that which is too big to embrace with reason alone. Our era is to a large degree characterized by rebellion against traditions. The newest and latest is rewarded and valued higher than that which is old. People like to imagine freedom as a state where there are no orders or given forms to keep; everything happens spontaneously according to one's own thoughts and inspiration. But the order that God has given us is not to limit life but, on the contrary, it is that which makes real freedom possible. In the house where I am now sitting and writing, there is a structure of load-bearing beams and pillars. They stabilize the building so that I can feel secure and write in peace and tranquility without fearing the roof and walls will suddenly fall in on me. These beams and walls do not occupy my attention; I take them for granted and do not even think about their presence. However, had the building been poorly constructed and the instability of the house could cause it to fall in, suddenly questions concerning structure and order become very important. It is similar with the church's order and structure; without them, confusion and chaos rule, and great injury can happen.

In many of his letters, Paul referred to the order that he himself has established and handed over to the congregations. Most likely, he was referring to a framework for sound teaching and a given content of the faith, the celebration of the divine service and the Christian life. When he could no longer be present himself, it was precisely these customs he referred to and reminded them of.

> For though I am absent in body, yet I am with you in spirit, rejoicing to see your good order and the firmness of your faith in Christ. Therefore, as you received Christ Jesus the Lord, so walk in him, rooted and built up in him and established in the faith, just as you were taught, abounding in thanksgiving (Col. 2:5–7).

That is why I sent you Timothy, my beloved and faithful child in the Lord, to remind you of my ways in Christ, as I teach them everywhere in every church (1 Cor. 4:17).

Exegetes usually point out that the letters of the New Testament are situational. Paul did not write compendiums where he presented abstract theological dogmas, but he gave answers to specific problems that came up in the congregations. These problems arose from different situations where there had been a sliding away from the center and where this order that Paul had handed over to the congregations had been distorted. Against this background of the New Testament's instruction and the good tradition, every Christian generation needs to watch over their theology and their order. The Christian church needs both reformation and tradition. Some see these as counterparts to each other, but tradition and reformation belong together. The reformers in the sixteenth century wanted to restore and preserve the church's true tradition, such as it had been given over to the church of the apostles and administered during the first centuries of the church. What was wanting of correction were abuses and aberrations of different sorts. There was no need to reject the tradition as such. When the church gives up the tradition "such as the faith once and for all entrusted to the saints" (Jude 3), God sends prophets and reformers who call the church to repentance and to once again return to the original sources. So, the question is not whether the church ought to stand on a tradition, but rather what the contents of this tradition are, if the tradition is good and promotes the gospel or if distortions of it have sneaked in.

The great Christian traditions flow like a river of the Spirit in the church through its two-thousand years of history. This stream never dwindles; it always finds new paths where men attempt to hinder this flood. There is something like a spiritual DNA in the body of Christ; the church is not itself if it seeks to oppose its own genes. A person can even say that when it is without abuse and distortion, tradition is the incarnation of Scripture in the life of the church. To affirm the value of tradition means nothing more than to confess the miraculous work that Christ has carried out in and through the history of the church. There is then a measuring stick for the tradition of the church, and it is Scripture. All traditions must be tested against Scripture, and that which stands in opposition against Scripture must be rejected. Even those who pride themselves in the reformational slogan Sola Scriptura—Scripture Alone—must hold to tradition. For the reformers, the content of the confession of the Scriptures is then not Sola Scriptura; that is to say that every Christian alone can create his own theology with the help of the Bible. For the reformers, Sola Scriptura meant that the Bible is the highest and final authority for teaching and life, but not the only authority. To affirm and preserve the true and good tradition is to confess: we are not the first generation of Christians; we build upon the foundation that is laid. While we reject misconceptions, we will carefully administer the wealth. We were not the first, we do not know best, and we have not come the furthest. The evangelical and reformational attitude toward tradition proceeds from a center that builds upon the instruction of the Bible: nothing is needed for man's salvation and justification but the gospel. But we can and shall thankfully receive all the gifts of wisdom and experience that the church inherited through the centuries, when they are in harmony with and promote the gospel.

The Reformation as a Reclamation of Evangelical Catholicity

To be eager for the Church's reformation does not mean that we want to get rid of our catholic inheritance but rather we seek to rediscover, regain, and restore this inheritance. It is a popular misunderstanding that the Reformation that proceeded from Wittenberg broke with all the orders and traditions of the church. Yet it is enough to refute this misunderstanding with some brief excerpts from the Augsburg Confession's summary:

> This is nearly a complete summary of the teaching among us. As can be seen, there is nothing here that departs from the Scriptures or the catholic church or from the Roman church . . . Nevertheless, the ancient rites are, for the most part, diligently observed among us. For the accusation is false that all ceremonies and ancient ordinances are abolished in our churches . . . Since the churches among us do not dissent from the catholic church in any article of faith, but only set aside a few abuses that are new and were accepted because of corruption over time . . . This was done in order that it may be understood that nothing has been accepted among us, in teaching or ceremonies, that is contrary to Scripture or the catholic church.[6]

So, from Luther and the Reformation we can find guidance concerning how to reclaim what is called universal common Christianity and rediscover what evangelical catholicity means. That is, a restoration of that which is abused or has been lost in the history of the church. In this sense, the word catholic deals with the rich and extensive church life that has been inherited from generation to generation. The church has received and taken over words, terms, patterns, and guidelines for how to perform baptism and celebrate the Lord's Supper, what a pastor should preach and how to give absolution, how to ordain priests and pastors, and many other valuable things. So, catholicity consists of both a universal content and a specific expression of the Christian faith. In the church, we often surprisingly encounter the same prayers and orders wherever we are in the world and at whatever time we search the history of the church. In his work *Christ's Church*, Bo Giertz paid attention to three different early church fathers: Irenaeus, Tertullian, and Clement of Alexandria.[7] Despite their different backgrounds, contexts, and languages, these figures give a consistent picture of what the faith and life of the church looked like during the second century. The first was a Greek from Asia Minor who became bishop of Lyon (present-day France). The second was African and served the church in Carthage. The third was active in Egypt and Palestine. We stand side by side with these three witnesses and other theologians, reformers, and martyrs of the church in our ministry in the church today. When the catholic inheritance and order of the church seem foreign to us, it is perhaps most often because the words and instructions of the Holy Scriptures themselves have become fundamentally foreign to us. Only when we are well anchored in the testimony of the Scriptures can we recognize and distinguish God's work in the past. It is not seldom that those who turn against the historic inheritance of the church have in actual fact also traded the Word of God for the secular currents and ideas of our time.

Luther's desire to establish genuine catholicity is not built upon an exceptional interpretation of Christianity that only the Lutherans hold. Luther's deepest intentions are recognized today, even within the

Roman Catholic context. For example, the document "From Conflict to Unity,"[8] signed by both Roman Catholics and Lutherans, notes that "Luther had no intention of establishing a new church, but was part of a broad and multifaceted desire for reform." Unlike Zwingli and Calvin, Luther did not break with the inheritance of the church, and, for that matter, neither did Thomas Cranmer of the Anglican Church. Remember that Martin Luther was not a Lutheran but rather "a good Catholic Christian, yes in actual fact a far better Catholic than the church leaders he criticized," as Peter Halldorf so strikingly expresses it.[9] This same striving for catholicity seen in Luther is also a clear emphasis in the Order of the (Lutheran) Church of Sweden. Bo Giertz wrote about this in the book *Christ's Church*:

> Distinguishing herself from these opposite traditions [Roman Catholic and Reformed, the Church of Sweden] our church wants to be both truly evangelical and truly catholic. [. . .] We can under no circumstances diverge from Scripture and its message of salvation. We count as one of the most unalienable treasures of Christianity the truth on justification by faith as Paul preached and Luther again brought to light. But these documents declare on the other hand just as clearly that we in no way have formed a new church but that we remain a branch of the church catholic.[10]

Thus, the reformers did not reinvent everything from the beginning and would not break from the tradition of the church. They wanted to reestablish the genuine evangelical tradition. So, to a great degree, they kept the church sanctuaries, the liturgy, the mass, the sign of the cross, church ordinances—yes, everything that advanced the proclamation of the gospel, or at least did not obscure the gospel. In our Protestant phobia against everything mildly catholic, we have unfortunately lost many irreplaceable treasures of the church's inheritance by neglecting the catholicity of the church. Gustaf Aulén, the great theologian of the Lund School and author of *Christus Victor*, was opposed to the word "Protestant" and chose instead to speak of the church's three catholic branches: the Greek Catholic, the Roman Catholic, and the Evangelical Catholic. For example, Aulén wrote the following: "He who has once had his eyes opened to what evangelical Christianity really means is thereby immune to the lure of Rome. We gladly recognize that Roman Christianity possesses great spiritual riches and stands for important values, even such as have often been unduly undone within Evangelical Christianity."[11] Instead, we find the great break with the church's catholicity in the new Protestantism and "cultural Christendom" that began during the eighteenth century. At that time church art was whitewashed and the liturgy truncated. The Lord's Supper became evermore rare and finally fell into oblivion. The average contemporary Protestant too often turns away from such things that, according to the reformers, belonged to the church's great treasure and were seen as common Christian property.[12]

Giertz writes, "It has accurately been said that if the gulf between Rome and Wittenberg was only a few yards, then the distance between the authentic evangelical faith and the neo-protestant cultural religion equals the distance between sun and moon."[13] Should the reformers be able to see the condition of the church as it is today, they would certainly call for reformation again. The position that Protestantism finds itself in today is certainly not what the reformers fought for. It has also been said, and I think that there is a lot to it: "When the evangelicals accuse you of being way too catholic, and the Catholics accuse you of being all too evangelical, then you can be sure that you are a Wittenberg Lutheran faithful to the Reformation." The Swedish author Fredrika Bremer expressed this similarly when she visited Pope Pius IX in 1859. In a conversation with a cardinal who said that a person like her ought not die as a heretic, she said, "I am no heretic. I am a catholic Christian." When the cardinal replied, "but not a Roman Catholic?" Fredrika Bremer answered, "No, I regard myself far more catholic than that!"[14]

Gunnar Rosendal, better known as Father Gunnar, was an eccentric Lutheran pastor from Osby in northeastern Skåne, who has meant a lot for evangelical catholicity in Sweden. He became a pioneer for the establishment of evangelical catholicity in the twentieth century with his example and program for church renewal. He thought that the word catholic must be re-appropriated even by the evangelicals, very simply because our churches should be able to regain a true understanding of themselves. As Father Gunnar expressed it: "This expresses something that cannot be said with any other word. We must incorporate precisely this word, not synonyms or parallels and glosses, the actual word 'catholic' must be re-incorporated into our language."[15]

Reclaim and Restore, Renew and Reconcile

Isolation and distancing attitudes mean that we miss these blessings, while networking and fellowship across borders lead us closer to the center, a community where we will be able to build the church in the light of the pure gospel upon the common foundation of the church according to the framework of tradition. As members of the same body, we are members of one another for service and support. Every limb has a particular task, which should not be streamlined and isolated, but which shall contribute to the health and function of the whole body. The body is of course the sum of its parts and can accomplish its purpose under the leadership of the head, but if one member suffers, the whole body suffers. A dynamic is then created in which seeking a return to the sources goes hand in hand with updating in the church. Thus, to reclaim and restore is, at the same time, to renew. Peter Halldorf notes that "when the church is at her best, she is deeply traditional and boldly creative."[16] In the same spirit, all the nineteenth-century awakenings in Sweden were inner-church movements that did not want to break with the church. Even the legendary Lewi Pethrus, the first leader of the Swedish Pentecostal movement, never wanted to leave the Church of Sweden. In a conversation with Bishop Manfred Björkqvist in 1946, he described the Pentecostals as a spiritual renewal movement within the Church of Sweden.[17]

Today, both traditional churches as well as all the non-denominational churches are characterized by a growing sense of rootlessness and restlessness. There are few events that are as destructive as to cut your own roots because then a man shuts himself off from his origin and opens himself to an existence without identity. Historical continuity has always been central to the people of God. The first Christians did not see themselves as founders of a new religion but as the completion of God's promise to his people, the promise that had a long history. The new covenant was a completion and renewal of this people that God had dealt with since the days of Abraham. So, our roots as Christ's church go much further back than to the days of the Apostles. Through Christ, we have been ingrafted into God's own people, and, in this way, the whole biblical history of salvation has also become our history.

When we reconnect to our own history, we receive great wealth. With his "Herdabrev" (Shepherd's Letter) of 1949, Bo Giertz said it this way:

> If one wants to see what true Christianity means or wants to learn how Christ's church lives and works, and know how a man is saved—then one should, above all, go back to the Apostles, Martyrs, and the days of the Church fathers. He should then set himself down and contemplate the message of the reformation, and finally he should not forget the favored seelsorgers[18] that God gave our church in the past century (the nineteenth) and through whom he gave us the deep awakenings of the church, from which all later generations have something to learn. It is this threefold inheritance, the early church, the reformation, and the awakenings, that should be administered and brought to life at this time. This means both to preserve and pass on, both to teach about the past and make it alive in the present. So this is our program: to teach about the past in order to be able to meet tomorrow, to dive so far down into the depths of the Church's great river of life that we are prepared to proclaim Christ's words to a new generation and before new men.[19]

So, we have a great and rich inheritance to reclaim and restore, renew and reconcile, from the whole history of God's people in the days of the Bible through the early church, the church fathers, the Reformation, and on to the present-day churches. This spiritual life pulsates through the body of Christ. The inheritance of the whole church belongs to us, or as Paul expresses it: "all is yours" (1 Cor. 3:22). Therefore, as modern Christians, we need to learn to live with a both/and, rather than an either/or. With such an attitude, a much greater and spacious world opens itself up in contrast to the cramped existence that labels, boxes, and pigeonholes create. If we refine ourselves as "the new thing God does" and start over again every time God sends renewal, we miss out on the accumulated riches of the church and blow the renewal the church needs so badly. There is enormous knowledge and wealth found within the body of Christ, and we do well to make it our own. These are treasures that surpass our individual understanding and are only applicable in communion with all the saints everywhere and throughout all generations.

"That you, being rooted and grounded in love, may have strength to comprehend with all the saints what is the breadth and length and height and depth, and to know the love of Christ that surpasses knowledge, that you may be filled with all the fullness of God" (Eph. 3:17b-19).

CHAPTER 2

Christianity's (Divinely Instituted) Means of Grace

Concerning the Sacramental Nature of the Church

Likewise, they teach that human beings cannot be justified before God by their own powers, merits, or works. But they are justified as a gift on account of Christ through faith when they believe that they are received into grace and that their sins are forgiven on account of Christ, who by his death made satisfaction for our sins. God reckons this faith as righteousness (Rom. 3 and 4).

So that we may obtain this faith, the ministry of teaching the gospel and administering the sacraments as through instruments the Holy Spirit is given, who effects faith where and when it pleases God in those who hear the gospel, that is to say, in those who hear that God, not on account of our own merits but on account of Christ, justifies those who believe that they are received into grace on account of Christ. Gal. 3: "So that we might receive the promise of the Spirit through faith."[1]

To Rightly Administer the Mysteries of God

The Apostle Paul spoke of himself and his coworkers as "servants of Christ and stewards of the mysteries of God" (1 Cor. 4:1). The same commission has been entrusted to all who serve as pastors and priests in Christ's church. A servant of Christ has in the deepest sense nothing else to present, speak about, or offer, other than Christ and him crucified (1 Cor. 2:2). The mystery does not refer to anything obscure or strange but to the gospel of Jesus Christ (Eph. 3:1–13). That the gospel is a mystery that has now been revealed means that the gospel of Jesus Christ had not been revealed in earlier generations in the same way that it has now been made known through the apostles of Christ. God's plan for the redemption of the world, which he had since before the creation of the world (Eph. 4:1–14), has now been revealed through the proclamation of the gospel. So, the mystery is associated with the divine, something that in its deepest sense is beyond human ability to comprehend and control. This mystery of the gospel is promoted and conveyed to us through specific means: the proclamation of the Word and the two sacraments, baptism and the Lord's Supper. For this reason, these means are commonly called the means of grace. These are the ways, the distribution channels, through which God is present and conveys his grace to us. These mysteries of grace run like red threads in the gospel of Jesus Christ. The incarnation—that God's Son is born as a man of flesh and blood—is a mystery. The cross—that he suffered and died as the sacrificial lamb that takes away the sin of the world—is a mystery. The empty tomb—that he rose and conquered the power of death—is a mystery. In the same way, the mediation of Christ to us today is a mystery. The Word—that Christ is present, speaks, and works through the preached word today—is a mystery. Baptism—that we die and rise again with Christ through baptism in water and are united with and sealed in Him—is a mystery. The Lord's Supper—that, through simple bread and wine, we participate in his body which is given for us and his blood shed for us for the forgiveness of sins—is a mystery.

Through these means of grace, God awakens faith in our hearts and Christ's righteousness is imputed to us sinners so that we stand completely justified before God. What a mystery! These holy features called sacraments are not ends in themselves but means through which God deals with us. As we read in the passage of the Augsburg Confession above: "That man cannot be justified before God by their own powers, merits or works, but they are justified as a gift on account of Christ through faith . . . so that we shall receive this faith, the ministry of the proclamation of the gospel and the administration of the sacraments has been instituted. For through the Word and sacraments, as through means, the Holy Spirit is given who effects faith in them who hear the gospel where and when it pleases God" [my paraphrase]. When Christ came into the world, he came in a visible and earthly form. He did not come as an abstract spiritual being, unbound by time and space, but in a human body. He is described by the Apostle John as the Word that became flesh and blood and took his dwelling among us. The effect of this was that men could see and experience his glory (John 1:14). So, Christ came to us in a physical way. As John writes in his first letter: "That which was from the beginning, which we have heard, which we have seen with our eyes, which we looked upon and have touched with our hands, concerning the word of life" (1 John 1:1). But for most, this glory was not revealed but hidden behind Christ's human form. Many rejected him because of his human and poor appearance. But there, in the midst of human weakness and insignificance, God himself was present among us.

So, through Christ, the grace of God and his presence is revealed in physical form. Divine power was carried in and operated through human words when, through his lips, Jesus spoke the forgiveness of sins to man. Diseases were healed when he laid his physical hands upon the sick. And, in the same way, Christ continues to be present in his body—the church—through the means he instituted. The means of grace convey the same efficacious word and power for the forgiveness, liberation, and restoration of the sinner even today. Yet just as Christ was rejected by many on the basis of his human appearance, so these means of grace are often neglected today. Many look for something that is experienced as more relevant or appealing to contemporary men. In other contexts, people chase after that which appears to be more spiritual than the grace of God mediated through Word, bread, and wine. But God has chosen to convey his presence through these means. Through the means of grace, God effectively mediates his promise and good gifts to us, and we receive them in faith. In fact, they are not particularly impressive to the eye, but in all their insignificance, they proclaim the mystery of faith and hand over the goods.

How Salvation Was Achieved for Us and Is Mediated to Us

In order to attain a deeper understanding of that which is called Christianity's means of grace, we need to rightly distinguish between how Christ acquired our salvation for us and how he now mediates it to us. Our salvation is not achieved by our partaking in the means of grace; their role is only to mediate that which Christ once and for all won for us on the cross of Calvary. Thus, the means of grace are distribution channels for God's grace. It is on the cross that Christ acquired the world's salvation, the sinner's forgiveness, redemption, and justification before God. But it is in the church that Christ mediates these blessings through his means of grace. The punishment was laid upon Christ so that we would receive peace, as we read in the fifty-third chapter of Isaiah. Upon Christ's cross, all sins have been gathered together and received their condemnation, and from Christ, grace floods out into the world through these means and channels. Therefore, the church's commission is to celebrate, proclaim, and mediate this salvation that Christ has acquired once and for all. "Where can I find a gracious God?" This was the question with which Luther ignited the Reformation, and it found its answer not in private spiritual experiences, but through the grace that is proclaimed and mediated through the Word, the table, and baptism. God has given these means of grace to the church. In Luther's own words:

> We treat the forgiveness of sins in two ways. First, how it is achieved and won. Second, how it is distributed and given to us. Christ has achieved it on the cross, it is true. But he has not distributed or given it on the cross. He has not won it in the supper or the sacrament. There he has distributed and given it through the Word, as also in the gospel, where it is preached. He has won it once for all on the cross. But the distribution takes place continuously, before and after, from the beginning to the end of the world . . .
>
> If now I seek the forgiveness of sins, I do not run to the cross, for I will not find it given there . . . But I will find in

the sacrament or gospel the word which distributes, presents, offers, and gives to me that forgiveness which was won from the cross.[2]

This is really good news for us. We are not referred to our own works, and we are not encouraged to turn our vision inward to find the presence of God. Salvation has an objective basis and is mediated to us through concrete means to which God has tied his promise. We can seek our comfort here and find it, completely independent of our occasional emotional mode or piety. Here Luther gives us valuable guidance. When he grappled with doubt, he set himself under the proclamation of the Word; he took his refuge in baptism. In the fight against sin, he went to confession. In the fight against the fear of death, he fled to the mass and the Lord's Supper. This is not hocus pocus, rather an attitude that finds its power through God's Word and promise, which envelops the sacraments and gives them meaning and effectiveness. It is the Word, visible in water, bread, and wine that is presented to us in a concrete way to be received in faith. Through the sacrament, God's grace takes form and embodies the central content of the gospel.

It is also on this point that all ideas concerning Luther as a cataclysm for modern individualism fail. It was completely foundational for Luther that it is the church that extends the gospel to the individual through the Word and sacraments in the divine service. So, the church is absolutely crucial for the Christian life that Luther describes. Every believer needs to be part of this assembly called the local church, where these gifts are handed to him from the outside. It is someone else that has baptized me. It is the mouth of another that speaks God's promises to me. The bread and wine are handed to me through someone else who simultaneously speaks the wonderful promise: "Given for you/shed for you." Thus, my subjective reception of grace requires the objective and firm foundation upon which it rests. This is the very sacramental nature of the church. And it is in this churchly and sacramental milieu that even Protestant Christendom has its origin, not the individualistic private Christianity where one emphasizes the "personal relationship to Jesus" as that which constitutes the Christian life. Against this background, a person might wonder whether Luther would consider some of today's Protestant congregations to be Christian churches in any significant way.

Secularizing and Sacralizing

So, the sacramental dimension deals with how God has tied his promise of salvation to external means: to Word, water, bread, and wine. The greatest enemies of sacramental Christianity are perhaps secular worldliness and the enthusiastic spirituality of those whom Luther called "schwermer," i.e., enthusiasts or fanatics. Both secularism and spirituality can manifest themselves in many different forms and expressions. Let me briefly mention a few core features. Secular worldliness emphasizes that the world is all there is. If God should find a place in one's life, then the spirituality must be relegated to the private and inner sphere. Rational reason must rule everything else. This way of thinking has even slipped into the church. That which was considered to be holy and set apart for God in earlier times today tends to be considered from a pragmatic point of view or assessed from a more rationalistic and short-term, market-based aspect. The approach has become: does this give us anything? Does it work? Does it get results?

Is there a demand? If not, then we take it away and exchange it for something more suitable that better serves our expectations. Sacred is what we call something set apart for God and holy. Today, sacred is perhaps associated mostly with something formal or strictly religious, in the very worst sense of the word. But the sacred is quite simply contrasted with the secular. The cure for the secularization of the church is therefore sacralization.[3] Here the sacraments play a central role. A sacramental understanding is not limited strictly to baptism, the Lord's Supper, and the preaching in the divine service; rather, it will come to define how an individual relates to the Christian faith in its totality. Sacramental theology takes its point of departure in the fact that God makes use of the created to reveal himself and meet his people. So, the gospel is expressed sacramentally in word and deed.

The spirituality of the fanatics is something that has threatened the gospel in every generation when men elevate their own spiritual experiences above God's Word. The Gnostics, with their distaste for the bodily and earthly, were the foremost internal enemies of the early church. But the Gnostics and their spiritualistic features have continued to challenge the church's sacramental theology. In his day, Luther called them *schwärmer* (swarmers), *übergeistlich* (hyper-spiritual), and *überchristlich* (hyper-Christians). From schwermeristic hyper-spirituality flows both an excessive mysticism and an unhealthy charismatic understanding, both of which have in common that they turn one's search for justification and piety inward. People want to have spiritual experiences and revelations "in the heart." They turn against the physical and ordinary and chase after the spectacular. Spirituality then becomes an end in itself and entirely detached from the gospel as an external word from God. Among other things, the Reformation has been accused—wrongly—of being the fountainhead of this subjective individualism. However, rather than overemphasizing the subjective and personal aspect of faith, the reformers consistently turned their gaze outward to the objective words of promise that are mediated through the Scriptures and sacraments.

> In these matters, which concern the spoken, external word, it must be firmly maintained that God gives no one his Spirit or grace apart from the external Word which goes before. We say this to protect ourselves from the enthusiasts [schwermer], that is, the "spirits," who boast that they have the Spirit apart from and before contact with the Word . . . Therefore we should and must insist that God does not want to deal with us human beings, except by means of his external Word and sacrament.[4]

Jesus Christ is the original and initial sacrament. Through the incarnation, God's Son occupied the womb of a woman and was born as a man to make God's invisible presence and grace visible in the world. Through the sacrifice of his physical body and blood, God has brought salvation for us. God is always present and free to operate precisely how, when, and where he wills. Yet the visible form—the sacraments—is for the sake of our weak faith. Therefore, we can always trust that God is present and operative in the sacraments precisely as he has promised. Without the Word, the sacraments are empty symbols. We will remain ignorant of what we access in the sacraments unless the Word is proclaimed. In and of themselves, without God's promise, they have no power. They are means and channels through which Christ, along with the Holy Spirit, gives himself to us. So, Christ and all his blessings reach you and me through the sacraments. It is not something we do for God, but God who gives something to us. Through faith, we receive God's good gifts in all these forms.

A Christianity operating by the means of grace is a Christianity for the weak, for those who feel unspiritual and who wrestle with temptations and *anfechtung* of different sorts. This is liberating for people who are pressured by the heavy burdens and demands placed on their inner faith to feel and experience. What such weary believers need is something that makes faith concrete, visible, and physically tangible. The sacramental dimension of the divine service is then a lifebuoy that drags them into the grace and love of God. So, God constantly comes to us to be encountered through the tangible and concrete means of grace. These are the nourishments of faith that bring life and fan the flickering flame of faith. So, let us never forget that the sacraments are instituted for our sake and not for God's. They become a sign of assurance for us that we have received the promise of God. A visible and real sign that we receive in faith. As was said before, in and of itself, the sign is nothing, but it is the promise that is bound to this sign that makes it effective. In this world, we relate to and orient ourselves with our physical senses. In our everyday lives, we use many material signs that are connected to deeper contents that remind us and assure us of what we have: wedding rings, bank cards and driver's licenses, security papers and contracts. When God deals with us through the sacraments, he does something similar. But an immaterial (gnostic) Christianity will always try to sneak in and reduce the mysteries of faith to an idea, a thought, an abstract spirituality that only deals with the heart. But immaterial assets are always hard to identify and capture, so this leads to ambiguity and uncertainty.

How We Recognize and Experience Christ's Presence

What I wrote above becomes obvious for us from the account in Luke's gospel about the two despairing disciples on their way to Emmaus. They are filled with grief. They were convinced that Jesus was dead and that everything was over. They gave up hope and were determined to move on. Their world had been shaken and everything was in anxious chaos. The events did not evolve according to their expectations. The only thing left was a feeling of emptiness and that everything was over. How many times have we ourselves not been there? The answers to our prayers never materialized. Our plans came to nothing. That which we believed in so strongly is something we now doubt. We cannot perceive God's presence, but rather we feel rejected and betrayed by God. Perhaps we got it completely wrong?

> That very day two of them were going to a village named Emmaus, about seven miles from Jerusalem, and they were talking with each other about all these things that had happened. While they were talking and discussing together, Jesus himself drew near and went with them. But their eyes were kept from recognizing him (Luke 24:13–16).

Yet there in the midst of all the confusion, Jesus is present. We cannot comprehend it with our senses, and we do not recognize him from our own thoughts concerning how he should come to us. The Bible begins in the same way. Everything was void, empty, and dark; everything was in chaos. But there was God. The Spirit brooded over the chaos. Suddenly, the Word sounded, and the darkness was evicted by light. Order stepped forth out of the chaos. That which had previously been deserted now teems with life. In his description of the Emmaus disciples, Luke highlights the very things—the means—that cause the disciples to recognize Christ. When they reflect upon the events, they say: "Did not our hearts burn within us when he spoke to us on the way, and opened to us the scriptures?" (Luke 24:32) and, "When he was at table with them, he took the bread and blessed and broke it and gave it to them. And their eyes were opened, and they recognized him" (Luke 24:30–31). God has weaved a picture of Christ through every page of Scripture. It was this that Christ himself showed the Emmaus disciples when he opened the Scriptures for them.

The entire Bible leads up to this: Jesus Christ died in our place and was sacrificed for our sin. Every page and every verse set the stage for this precious message of salvation—the gospel! This is how we recognize Christ's presence. It is through the Word and sacraments that he reveals himself and comes to us from without. It is this and only this that makes the church Christ's church and therefore makes us the body of Christ. When, through the Word, we hear him speak to us. When, in baptism, we are buried to be united with him in his death and resurrection. When, in the bread and wine of the Lord's Supper, we participate in his body and blood. All of this happens through the Holy Spirit, who works through these external means. The church mediates the forgiveness of sins, all the blessings of Christ, and gives us life overflowing in abundance, through these means of grace.

In two places, Paul refers to what he himself received from the Lord. He strongly emphasizes that this deals with what is most important and absolutely central for our Christian faith and the life of the church. This is the center of redemption that is proclaimed and manifested in the Scriptures and sacraments, distributed through the preaching in the pulpit and the gifts on the table.

> For I delivered to you as of first importance what I also received: that Christ died for our sins in accordance with the Scriptures, that he was buried, that he was raised on the third day in accordance with the Scriptures (1 Cor. 15:3–3).

> For I received from the Lord what I also delivered to you, that the Lord Jesus on the night when he was betrayed took bread, and when he had given thanks, he broke it, and said, "This is my body, which is for you. Do this in remembrance of me." In the same way also he took the cup, after supper, saying, "This cup is the new covenant in my blood. Do this, as often as you drink it, in remembrance of me." For as often as you eat this bread and drink the cup, you proclaim the Lord's death until he comes (1 Cor. 11:23–26).

So, in the interest in emphasizing the marks of the church and in my eagerness to see a reformation of the church, I am concerned in the deepest sense with how we can know for sure where we can meet Christ, and how he mediates his grace and gives the forgiveness of sins to us. The angels greeted the women at the grave on Easter morning: "You seek Jesus the crucified. He is not here. He has risen" (Mark 16:6). Yet if he is not there, if he is not in the grave or on the cross, where then is he? Where can we meet him? Perhaps with a little imagination and with the help of the knowledge we have received from the New Testament, we can hear the angels tell us: "He is not here, but he is there, in the Word and sacraments, precisely as he said and promised."

CHAPTER 3

Charismatic

Concerning the Church's Gifts of Grace

Christ the resurrected, the glorified, the ascended, who transcends time and space and is present in his church. In every
moment the border between eternal and temporal, heaven and
earth is pierced. The whole time Christ comes and is present
in his body which is the church and this presence is made visible through the pneumatic reality that the Spirit creates in the
Word and the sacraments. The whole time Christ's life flows
in the church and takes form in people. In the church, time
and space are transcended by his constant presence. The vision
is to see this transcendent reality present here and now: the
transcendent as a lifeline and Christ is in the center. Christ,
the means of grace, and those who are sanctified through the
means of grace, Christ's body, God's people, a spiritual life that
takes form in people—this is Giertz's vision of the church.[1]

The Century of the Holy Spirit

To be a Christian is to participate in the life of the Holy Spirit who emanates from the gospel and flows through the means of grace. So, all Christians become "living stones" who are "being built up as a spiritual house" (1 Pet. 2:5), where we "serve each other, as each has received a gift of grace, as good stewards of God's varied grace" (1 Pet. 4:10). Therefore, the whole Christian life is a life in the power of the Holy Spirit. Jesus speaks about this in the following way: "Whoever believes in me, as the Scripture has said, 'Out of his heart will flow rivers of living water.' Now this he said about the Spirit, whom those who believed in him were to receive, for as yet the Spirit had not been given, because Jesus was not yet glorified" (John 7:38–39). It is not my intention to present a complete doctrine of the Spirit in this chapter. The focus of this book is on the marks of the church, but as an introduction and because of my background as a Pentecostal pastor, I briefly want to address my current view on the charismatic dimension and how I understand the presence of the Spirit and his activity in and through Christ's church.

In the third article of the creed, the church says: "We believe in the Holy Spirit, and in one Holy, Christian Church." So, the church is a work of the Spirit, and the people of God are a people of the Spirit. Despite this, a person could still possibly call this last century the century of the Holy Spirit. Not because the Holy Spirit has been inactive during the earlier history of the church, but during the twentieth century, we have been able to see the fire of the Pentecostal movement sweep over the entire world and the charismatic renewal find paths into the different historic churches. Today, it is estimated that there are around 600 million charismatic Christians. So, today the charismatic expression and the gifts of the Spirit are affirmed far outside the Pentecostal camps. The charismatic movement is, to a large degree, now found within traditional church bodies, not the least within the Roman Catholic church. These churches have not given any exclusivity to charismatic life alone; charismatic expressions exist side by side with the sacramental life.

We find testimonies of the charismatic life in early church history, not the least among the church fathers. There are descriptions of charismatic gifts that came into expression as a sign of God giving the gift of the Spirit in connection with the intercession for the newly baptized, in accord with what happened when Paul came to Ephesus (Acts 19:5–6).[2] Origen speaks about water baptism as a spring from which the gifts of the Spirit flow, an approach that seems to agree with the catholic Christian faith of that time.[3] Irenaeus, who was bishop of Lyon during the third century, says the following concerning the charismatic life: "We also hear that many brothers in the church have these gifts. They speak in all sorts of spirit-given tongues and in a healthy way bring to light that which is hidden from men and reveal God's mystery."[4] Both Augustine of Hippo, one of the church's greatest theologians, and St. Francis of Assisi, one of the church's most venerated saints, describe many supernatural miracles and signs in their writings. The charismatic aspect of the Christian life seems to have diminished as the church did away with and rejected various unhealthy movements that abused the gifts. Montanism, an early church-era movement started by a man named Montanus, is probably the most known movement. Montanus was eventually dismissed as a heretic for advocating all kinds of charismatic peculiarities, hard-driven asceticism, and prophetic speculations.[5] This danger is always found where one overemphasizes the charismatic and simultaneously diminishes the Scriptures, where one exalts in one's own spirituality and pulls away from the orthodoxy of faith. Yet the charismatic aspect of faith has never completely ceased in the history of the church, and, during the previous century, the embers were stoked and the whole church experienced renewal.

My spiritual roots are in the Swedish Pentecostal Movement. Today I would describe myself as an open, but cautious charismatic. I am no "cessationist," that is, a person who believes that gifts of the Spirit ceased after the days of the Apostles. I am a "continuationist," who believes that the gifts of the Spirit are continually bestowed upon the church throughout history. This proceeds from a theological conviction that I describe later on in this chapter, but also from my experience within a charismatic congregation. It is within the Pentecostal movement that the foundation of my spiritual life and service was laid and formed. Its emphasis on being filled by the Spirit has created a warm fellowship, passionate worship, and fiery prayers, fostering a devotion characterized by bold initiatives, but above all an eagerness for evangelism and missions. Surely, my experiences of the charismatic are mixed. There are still unhealthy inclinations and abuses in the wake of the charismatic movement. At the same time, there are few other contexts where I have witnessed such a beautiful and warm Christianity that is so eager for the expansion of God's kingdom. Here too it is not an either/or, but a both/and. Charismatic Christians must then be anchored in good theology and good catholic order; one cannot build a church on charismatic experience alone. Genuine spiritual renewal never happens at the expense of theological development. The same Spirit who gives us his overabundant life has also given us doctrine. Scripture and Spirit cannot be put in opposition to each other.

We learn from the first page of the Bible that God's Word and Spirit are not in conflict, that God created through the Word *and* the Spirit. "The earth was without form and void, and darkness was over the face of the deep. And the Spirit of God was hovering over the face of the waters. And God said, 'Let there be light,' and there was light" (Gen. 1:2–3). So, Jesus and the Spirit belong and go together. Jesus does nothing without the Spirit and the Spirit does nothing without Jesus. He was conceived by the Holy Spirit. Mary was informed by the angel that, "The Holy Spirit will come upon you, and the power of the Most High will overshadow you; therefore the child to be born will be called holy—the Son of God" (Luke 1:35). Jesus was baptized in the Jordan, and the Spirit testified by descending upon in him the form of a dove (Luke 3:22). Filled with the Holy Spirit, Christ was led out into the desert by the Spirit and returned in the power of the Spirit to Galilee after 40 days (Luke 4:1, 14). In the Synagogue in Nazareth, he read from the book of Isaiah, "The Spirit of the Lord is upon me, because he has anointed me to proclaim good news to the poor. He has sent me to proclaim liberty to the captives and recovering of sight to the blind, to set at liberty those who are oppressed, to proclaim the year of the Lord's favor" (Luke 4:18–19). And then proclaimed, "Today this Scripture has been fulfilled in your hearing" (Luke 4:21). With that, Jesus began his ministry in the power of the Spirit. Peter summarizes the ministry of Christ in the following way: "God anointed Jesus of Nazareth with the Holy Spirit and with power. He went about doing good and healing all who were oppressed by the devil, for God was with him" (Acts 10:38). The preaching of Jesus was different from that of the scribes: "And they were astonished at his teaching, for he taught them as one who had authority, and not as the scribes . . . A new teaching with authority!

He commands even the unclean spirits, and they obey him" (Mark 1:22, 27). Jesus suffered, died, and was buried, but God raised him from the dead by the Spirit (Rom. 8:11). He ascended to the right hand of the Father, and the Spirit descended upon the church (Christ's body). The apostles then carried out the great commission in the power of the Spirit (Acts 1:8; 3:29–31). So, the Spirit is active throughout the history of the church up to our day.

As I see it, there are four great streams within Christ's church: the Catholic, the Orthodox, the Evangelical (that is Lutheran), and the Charismatic. When these streams meet each other and are united, a river is formed with strong and rich floods that can give true renewal to the whole of Christ's church. This book revolves around the reformational and evangelical, but allow me to wade into the charismatic stream in this chapter.

Luther and the Charismatics

How can one then perceive the connection between the Lutheran tradition and the charismatic? Perhaps the charismatic has been underemphasized in Lutheran circles because of Luther's experience of those he called "Schwermers" and "enthusiasts," also described as "the fanatics." Here, Luther collided with a charismatic faith that was characterized by a spectacular spirituality in which people sought the Spirit's mediation apart from external means. With that, they ruined the place of the Word and sacraments as means of grace through which God works in the church. One of the fanatics and Radical Reformation's leaders, Thomas Müntzer, "rejected all baptisms and said that the Bible was nothing but paper and ink." He meant that, "The Spirit could give completely new revelations and came immediately without the Word," for example, "that one should hasten the arrival of the kingdom of God by killing all the ungodly."[6] Luther was understandably horrified by this idea. "What Luther reacted against was the conception of the Christian life where emotions ruled supreme, a sort of piety characterized by a theology of glory," writes Christian Braw.[7] The basic difference between the fanatics[8] and Luther applies to order. Luther placed the external mediation of the Word before the inner work, while the fanatics turned things around and took their point of departure from the Spirit's inner work freed from these external means. Luther wrote:

> Now when God sends forth his holy gospel he deals with us in a twofold manner, first outwardly, then inwardly. Outwardly he deals with us through the oral word of the gospel and through material signs, that is, baptism and the sacrament of the altar. Inwardly he deals with us through the Holy Spirit, faith, and other gifts. But whatever their measure or order the outward factors should and must precede. God has determined to give the inward to no one except through the outward.

For Luther, it is the gift of the Spirit that kills the old man and sanctifies the person in the likeness of Christ. For the fanatics, it is their own sanctification and conversion, their own chastening of the flesh and their pious deeds that are rewarded with the gift of the Holy Spirit. For Luther, the initiative always lies with God. We receive the Spirit's work as a gift of God. But the enthusiasts emphasize one's own faith and seeking after the Holy Spirit instead.[9]

Luther fought against abuse in the church on two fronts: on the one hand, against the sacramentalists, and on the other, against the fanatics. This historical background does not mean that we should do away with the charismatic. Just as we would not do away with the sacraments because the sacramentalists abused them, so we do not need to do away with the charismatic aspects of the faith because of the abuse of the fanatics. A person should not forget that Luther was strongly influenced by the mystics like Bernard of Clairvaux (1091–1153) and Johannes Tauler (1300–1361).[10] In "Concerning Councils and the Church," he criticizes "fine Easter preachers" because they are "poor Pentecost preachers, for they do not preach *'de sanctificatione et vivificatione Spiritus sancti,'* (concerning the sanctification and giving of life in the Holy Spirit) . . . so that the Holy Spirit may transform us out of the old Adam into new men . . ."[11] Luther even forms a spirituality that is somewhat similar to modern charismatics. He often speaks of the devil and demons, spiritual experiences and revelations. For example, when he instructs concerning prayer, he writes, "you must learn to cry out and not sit there for yourself on the bench . . . no, get up, you slacker, fall on your knees, lift your hands and eyes up to the heavens, read a psalm or the Our Father, and lay your distress out before God with tears if need be, complain and cry out to him."[12] Birgit Stolt creates this picture with her many years studying Luther's use of language in both his letters and table talks. In her book *Luther själv-hjärtats och glädjens teolog* (Luther, Theologian of the Heart and Joy), she notes that "in the reception of Luther's theology the intellectual aspect has unfortunately received much more attention than the emotional" and regrets that "the current (Swedish) picture of Luther is unique in the evangelical world."[13] In the chapter concerning how Luther spoke about and lived in prayer, a clear picture emerges of what I would label a charismatic in the best sense of the word. For Luther, prayer is the foremost place where we live out our faith by communicating with God, and where, through our meditation of Scripture, God talks to us through the enlightenment of the Holy Spirit.

Lutheran theology is therefore sound and stable ground for a both/and perspective, namely, that spirituality is both sacramental and charismatic. Therefore, a Lutheran cannot dismiss all charismatics as fanatics. Instead, the charismatic renewal needs to be firmly anchored in good evangelical and Lutheran theology to avoid overheated abuse, but Lutheran churches need charismatic warmth so as not to be dogmatic ice chests that resemble morgues more than they do hospitals. With a robust reformational theology embodied in a catholic church liturgy, where the Spirit is given through Word and sacraments, the work of the Spirit is displayed through charismatic gifts for the edification and growth of the church.

Today the Lutheran church is growing strongest in Africa. The Mekane Yesus Church in Ethiopia is the world's largest and fastest-growing Lutheran church body, and it is an example of a movement that unites good Lutheran theology and liturgy with the charismatic aspects of the faith. It is in this context that the *Confessio Augustana* is reprinted in great editions and is spread side by side with a charismatic warmth and boldness. For Luther, there was not a single area in the church and not a single theological aspect where the Holy Spirit's activity was not fundamental. The Spirit is present and active in and through everything God does in the world, or, to say it another way, all that God does happens in and by the Holy Spirit.[14] When Luther expounds on Galatians 3:5, "Does he who supplies the Spirit to you and works miracles among you," he writes the following:

It's as if he'd said, "It wasn't enough that God gave you the Spirit, but God Himself has also enriched you with the gifts of the Spirit and has given them growth. Thus once you received the Spirit, the Spirit would always grow, becoming more fruitful among you." Thus it is clear the Galatians had worked miracles, or at least had demonstrated the fruits of the faith that the disciples of the true Gospel will always display. In another place, Paul says, "Because the kingdom of God does not consist in words but in power." This power is not only the ease of words with which to talk about God's kingdom. It is also certainly true to show that God by means of His Spirit is effective in us.[. . .] It is well and good to love your neighbor so unselfishly that you would part with your money, goods, and even your eyes and all you have for your salvation and even more to suffer patiently adversity and affliction; all these indeed are powerful virtues of the Spirit. "All these powers," he says, "you have received and enjoyed." . . . However, you received these fruits not by the law but from God who suppled them to you, and the Spirit grew daily among you.[15]

Here, Luther touches on something central concerning the life of the Spirit. The Spirit is given through the proclamation of the Word and the sacraments administered and distributed according to the Lord's command. The Spirit wants to come to all and be manifested in the form of fruit and gifts. Paul says: "To each is given the manifestation of the Spirit for the common good" (1 Cor. 12:7). Thus, the fruit of the Spirit and gifts of grace are not means of grace, means through which the Spirit is given to us, but they are expressions of how the

Spirit works through us to serve our neighbor, for the edification of the congregation, and for the spread of the gospel. Even here, a distinction has to be made between the fruits of the Spirit and the Spirit's gifts. The Spirit's foremost task is to sanctify and mold us into the likeness of Christ. The fruit of the Spirit grows and matures when we live in faith in Christ. While the Spirit's fruit is a sign that one is a bearer of Christ's life, the Spirit's gifts are a manifestation of Christ's ministry. However, we should remember that a person recognizes a tree by its fruit. Jesus says that on the last day, people will come and point to their ministry and their great deeds, miracles, and signs that they carried out with the help of his name. But he will answer them: "I never knew you; depart from me, you workers of lawlessness" (Matt. 7:23).

So, genuine spirituality is not measured by our spiritual gifts but by the fruits of our lives: the likeness of Christ. A profound work of God is characterized by the Spirit's fruit which is "faith working through love" (Gal. 5:6), where we "but through love serve one another" (Gal. 5:13). And this is expressed in the form of "love, joy, peace, patience, kindness, goodness, faithfulness, gentleness, self-control" (Gal. 5:22–23). A tree that bears fruit does not make much noise about it, but when one tastes the fruit, one makes a big deal of it. So it is for the Christian too; for him, the fruit is in large part hidden, but it is perceived by his neighbor. Then neither fruit nor gift shall be described as a certificate or medal for faithfulness to Christ. It is rather the sign of God's great grace and his loving intervention in our lives. Let us now see what the Holy Spirit does in and through his church.

Neither you nor I could ever know anything about Christ or believe in him and receive him as Lord, unless these were offered to us and bestowed on our hearts through the preaching of the gospel by the Holy Spirit. The work is finished and completed; Christ has acquired and won the treasure for us by his sufferings, death, and resurrection. [. . .] For creation is now behind us, and redemption has also taken place, but the Holy Spirit continues his work without ceasing until the last day, and for this purpose he has appointed a community on earth, through which he speaks and does all his work. For he has not yet gathered together all of this Christian community, nor has he completed the granting of forgiveness. Therefore we believe in him who daily brings us into this community through the word, and imparts, increases, and strengthens faith through the same word and the forgiveness of sins.[16]

New Life

In the Nicene Creed, the Holy Spirit is called *the giver of life*. This new life that the good news of the gospel speaks about is given to us by God through that which I earlier called God's distribution channels: the preached Word and the administered sacraments. Therefore, to receive the Holy Spirit is synonymous with receiving the gifts of salvation: the forgiveness of sins and a righteousness through faith. The reception of the Spirit is thus not a "second step" that follows salvation, like a two-stage shebang. Paul confirms this when he asks the rhetorical question of the Galatians: "Did you receive the Spirit by works of the law or by hearing with faith?" (Gal. 3:2) The historical situation, behind which Galatians was written, was not concerned with how one was "baptized by the Spirit" but how one is saved. Is one saved through faith in Christ and keeping certain parts of the law, or is one saved by faith in Christ alone? This is the point of contention in Galatians. Thus, for Paul, it is the same thing to be saved, to come to faith, to be baptized in water and receive the Holy Spirit. Later in the same chapter, we read: "Christ redeemed us from the curse of the law by becoming a curse for us—for it is written, 'Cursed is everyone who is hanged on a tree'—so that in Christ Jesus the blessing of Abraham might come to the Gentiles, so that we might receive the promised Spirit through faith" (Gal. 3:13–14), and "for in Christ Jesus you are all sons of God, through faith. For as many of you as were baptized into Christ have put on Christ" (Gal. 3:26–27). This new life is a life in the power of the Holy Spirit, and the Holy Spirit is given to us through the means that God has instituted in his church: the Word and sacrament. When we believe in Christ, "we live by the Spirit" (Gal. 6:25), and "in one Spirit we were all baptized into one body—Jews or Greeks, slaves or free—and all were made to drink of one Spirit" (1 Cor. 12:13). So Spirit Baptism is nothing but the gift of salvation through faith and baptism. On the other hand, being filled by the Spirit, to let yourself be filled by the Holy Spirit is a continuous experience.

The Helper

When Jesus introduces the Spirit to his disciples, he speaks about him as *The Helper* "to be with you forever" (John 14:16–17). The Greek word is *parakletos*, which has the meaning to be sent out to be a help and support. Yet the word also had a more formal meaning and was used in the context of jurisprudence. The word hinted at a person who would assist and defend an accused person and plead their cause. A further meaning that William Barclay[17] has brought attention to is someone who "inspires soldiers to fight before a battle or inspires courage in them."[18]

A *parakletos* can also be a comforter, an interpreter, and a guide. Jesus is the one who has been with the disciples, and he has instructed them, helped and comforted them, defended them, given them courage and joy. In his farewell speech, he speaks about "another Helper," the Holy Spirit who shall always remain with them and be in them in order to continue this work. What is it then that we need more specific help with from the Holy Spirit?

In one sense, the Holy Spirit is our teacher. A good teacher adheres to doctrine, teaches it, and reminds people of it. Sometimes completely false and strange dichotomies are set up between the Spirit and Scripture, and life and doctrine. However, all Scripture is inspired by the Holy Spirit (2 Pet. 1:20–21; 2 Tim. 3:16). The Spirit enlightens and gives us insight through the proclamation of the Word and reminds us of the words of Jesus (John 14:26). The Spirit witnesses and points to Jesus, not to himself (John 15:26). When the Word is proclaimed, the Helper convicts people concerning sin and righteousness and judgment (John 16:8). He is the Spirit of truth and leads us step by step into the whole truth (John 16:13–14). So, without the Spirit's enlightenment, we cannot see or understand the truth (1 Cor. 2:4,12). So, Paul prays for the congregation in Ephesus that God will give them the "Spirit of wisdom and of revelation in the knowledge of him, having the eyes of your hearts enlightened, that you may know what is the hope to which he has called you, what are the riches of his glorious inheritance in the saints, and what is the immeasurable greatness of his power toward us who believe, according to the working of his great might" (Eph. 1:17–19). This great active power is nothing other than the Holy Spirit who is mediated through the channels that God has instituted— the means of grace.

Sonship

We have been adopted through faith and have received the status of children by God. We have become children of God and may call God our Father. Adoption, just like justification, is both a relational and legal term. Our status has been changed on a legal plan. We are no longer "sons of disobedience," we who "by nature were children of wrath" (Eph. 2:2–3). The Gospel of John hits this hard, "But to all who did receive him, who believed in his name, he gave the right to become children of God" (John 1:12). This is a legal reality, something the supreme judge has made firm and determined. Yet one can doubt this wonderful fact, not the least when we sometimes behave, think, and act as if we are still the devil's children (John 8:44). However, the Holy Spirit, whom God gave to us in baptism and that we have received in faith, witnesses to the fact that we are God's children (Rom. 8:1–16) This can also be made visible to us through the intercession and anointing with oil that in many traditions is commonly done in connection with baptism in water (Eph. 1:13).

Foretaste

Christmas and Easter lead to Pentecost. The goal of the incarnation and redemption is renewal. Through the miracle of Pentecost, we receive a foretaste of the new creation. The Spirit's giving is the sign that the new age has broken into our day, the new creation is here "already but not yet." Through the gift of the Spirit, we have received a foretaste of what awaits us; the future has broken into the present. We "have tasted the heavenly gift, and have shared in the Holy Spirit, and have tasted the goodness of the word of God and the powers of the age to come" (Heb. 6:4–5). The Jews who were with Peter in the house of Cornelius were shocked when they saw the Holy Spirit given to the Gentiles for two reasons: first, it means that the Spirit is not given to them who keep the law but by grace to those who believe the gospel. Second, it witnesses to the new age which has begun and that God's kingdom is here (Acts 10:45). The Spirit's presence is therefore a great comfort in the midst of the everyday agony in this world's fallen state—and a first fruits of the future redemption from the slavery and corruption that all of creation will experience at the return of Jesus (Rom 8:20–23; Eph. 1:14; 4:30).

Sanctification

The Holy Spirit makes us holy. The goal of God's salvation is to renew and rehabilitate everything. Men are created in God's image and intended to reflect his being. God has determined those whom he has called out of the world and in his congregation "to be formed according to his son's image" (Rom. 8:29). The Spirit carries out this work by killing the old man with all his sinful desires and deeds. When, in Ephesians, Paul speaks about "being imitators of God" (Eph. 5:1) and admonishes us seriously to "walk as children of light" (Eph. 5:8), he summarizes the counsel with these words: "Instead, let yourself be filled with the Spirit" (Eph. 5:18). So we need to abandon ourselves and cooperate with this renewal (Rom. 12:1–2) through a life of regular worship where we sit under the Lord's Word and come to the Lord's table, as well as through prayer and spiritual guidance, soul care, confession, and absolution. In the Eastern Church, tradition means nothing less than to "receive the divine nature" (2 Pet. 1:4). The Spirit carries out this work by being active in everyday temptations, tests, and exercises, and the fear of God and brotherly love, and then through different virtues, insights, self-control, and endurance (2 Peter 1:5–8). In Lutheran lingo, this is part of what is called the "Theology of the Cross" and the doctrine of vocation.

Prayer

A person could also call the Holy Spirit the Spirit of prayer. The Prophet Zechariah speaks about the Lord "pouring a spirit of grace and prayer" (Zech. 12:10) over his people. God desires communion with us, and the Spirit draws us into this intimate relationship with the whole Trinity (1 Cor. 1:9). The Spirit helps us in our weakness and guides us through the world of prayer, "For we do not know what to pray for as we ought, but the Spirit himself intercedes for us with groanings too deep for words. And he who searches hearts knows what is the mind of the Spirit, because the Spirit intercedes for the saints according to the will of God" (Rom 8:26–27). So, there is a constant prayer meeting within us because we are the temple of the Holy Spirit (1 Cor. 6:19), and we are encouraged to participate in the Spirit's prayer (Eph. 6:18, Jude 20). So, we may experience the Spirit giving us a new language of prayer. Tongues without interpretation is primarily a language of prayer that is to be used in one's private devotions (1 Cor. 14:2,4). Paul explains: "For if I pray in a tongue, my spirit prays but my mind is unfruitful . . . I will pray with my spirit, but I will pray with my mind also; I will sing praise with my spirit, but I will sing with my mind also . . . For you may be giving thanks well enough, but the other person is not being built up. I thank God that I speak in tongues more than all of you. Nevertheless, in church I would rather speak five words with my mind in order to instruct others, than ten thousand words in a tongue" (1 Cor. 14:14–15, 17–19).

Equipping

The Spirit equips us for our task here in the world. Jesus summarized what the gifts of the Spirit are for just before he ascended to heaven, saying: "You will receive power when the Holy Spirit has come upon you, and you will be my witnesses in Jerusalem and in all Judea and Samaria, and to the end of the earth" (Acts 1:8). The Spirit's presence and activity in the congregation is synonymous with a zeal for evangelism. The Spirit drives workers out into the world to both sow the gospel seed and gather the harvest. This happens at a high price amidst opposition and persecution. The word "witness" is "martyr" in Greek; it brings to mind those who received the task to die a martyr's death for their faith. Throughout the whole history of the church, men and women filled with the Holy Spirit have left comfort and security behind and risked their lives to proclaim the gospel to the unreached. It is this experience that Paul expresses with the words, "Christ's love compels us" (2 Cor. 5:14). One of the main ways that the Spirit equips the church is to give her different spiritual gifts and ministries (1 Cor. 12:11). Jesus seriously urged the disciples not to start the task before they had been "clothed with power from on high" (Luke 24:49). In the rest of this chapter, we will be taking a closer look at this power, these gifts and equipment.

Spiritual Gifts

While most Christians would likely concur with most of what I have said above, there are different opinions concerning the gifts of the Spirit. Paul is the only one who uses the word *charisma* in the New Testament, except for Peter, who uses it on one occasion: "As each has received a gift [spiritual gifts], use it to serve one another, as good stewards of God's varied grace" (1 Pet. 4:10). *Charisma* has the wider meaning of an undeserved gift given by grace alone. In a more specific meaning, it is used for the New Testament concept of spiritual gifts of grace. These gifts are special abilities that the Spirit reveals for the edification of the congregation. I will emphasize again that one must distinguish between the means of grace and spiritual gifts. It is through the means of grace that the forgiveness of sins is mediated and the Spirit is given. A conscience weighed down by sin and an uneasy soul shall not be guided or admonished to seek comfort in some spiritual experience or spiritual gifts. Peace with God cannot be built on spiritual experiences but only on the gospel's firm promise that comes through the proclamation of the Word, baptism in water, and the bread and wine of the Lord's Supper. The Spirit then does his work within us and works through our life by the fruit and gifts of the Spirit.

When Paul writes to the congregation in Corinth, he writes simultaneously to "all those who in every place call upon the name of our Lord Jesus Christ" (1 Cor. 1:2), and he continues by saying "the testimony about Christ was confirmed among you—so that you are not lacking in any gift, as you wait for the revealing of our Lord Jesus Christ" (1 Cor. 1:6–7). We can consider ourselves included in this greeting and expect that the Spirit will continue to give gifts to the church so that she may complete her commission in expectation of the Lord's return. It is important for Paul that the congregation be conscious of these gifts: "Now concerning these spiritual gifts, brothers, I do not want you to be uninformed" (1 Cor. 12:1). Not all believers possess all or the same gifts (1 Cor. 12:29–30), but we are admonished to seek and strive after the spiritual gifts (1 Cor. 12:31). However, we do not have dominion over the gifts, and we cannot decide who receives what, but the Spirit "shares his gifts to whom he wills" (1 Cor. 12:11), and "to each is given the manifestation of the Spirit for the common good" (1 Cor. 12:7). This "common good" means "building up the body of Christ, until we all attain to the unity of the faith and of the knowledge of the Son of God, to mature manhood, to the measure of the stature of the fullness of Christ . . . from whom the whole body, joined and held together by every joint with which it is equipped, when each part is working properly, makes the body grow so that it builds itself up in love (Eph. 4:12–13, 16). It is obvious that gifts should be understood and used in the collective community of the congregation. No gift is sufficient in and of itself, but all the different gifts are dependent upon the remaining members and functions of the body (1 Cor. 12:19–22).

There are many lists of different gifts in the New Testament—ministries and activities or works through which the Spirit reveals himself (1 Cor. 12:4–6). As I see it, these lists do not exist so we can tick off our own gifts or choose from a set and limited menu. Rather than prescriptive, it is more descriptive of the wealth of ways in which the Spirit reveals himself and works within the congregation. That God gave us the Spirit and equipped us will be expressed and revealed in many different ways depending on circumstances and need. Everything should be done with order and peace, grounded in the Scriptures for the edification of the congregation, "so that all are instructed and all are equipped" (1 Cor. 14:26–33). All gifts and works must endure test, examination, and reflection. "Do not quench the Spirit. Do not despise prophecies, but test everything; hold fast what is good" (1 Thess. 5:19–21). Some good advice I received as a young pastor from an older servant of the Lord was this: "The charismatic gifts of 1 Cor. 12 must first be baptized in the pure love of 1 Cor. 13, then be used according to the prescriptions of 1 Cor. 14 and always grounded in the message of 1 Cor. 15." When all this is said, we need to, above all, recognize and concentrate on the real work of the Spirit and not be paralyzed by imitations and abuses. Despite everything, Paul admonishes us to "pursue love and earnestly desire the spiritual gifts" (1 Cor. 14:1).

The charismatic congregational life is characterized by a faith in and expectation of God's noticeable presence, a bold belief in prayer, and a ministry to people with the expectation of God's supernatural intervention, healing, and deliverance, in which he performs signs and wonders. It is characterized by passionate reverence for God and a longing after God's powerful deeds. However, the work of the Spirit is always and above all a baptism in God's love, "because God's love has been poured into our hearts by the Holy Spirit who has been given to us" (Rom. 5:5). From this love of God springs that which characterizes the Spirit's work within us: the love for Jesus and all people (1 John 4:7–13). The Spirit's chief task is to glorify Jesus and draw people to him. For me, good charismatic characteristics are a hunger to dig deeper into God's Word, a love for God's people and Christ's church, a serious commitment to and engagement in congregational life, a yearning for prayer and an intense desire for evangelism. The life of the Spirit pours into the church through the means of grace. Let us therefore not neglect worship and church life, but as often as occasion permits, receive the Spirit's life and gifts through the gathering around the Lord's Word and the Lord's table. Therefore, fully trusting in the promise of Jesus, let us boldly pray for the Spirit's gifts: "For everyone who asks receives, and the one who seeks finds, and to the one who knocks it will be opened. What father among you, if his son asks for a fish, will instead of a fish give him a serpent; or if he asks for an egg, will give him a scorpion? If you then, who are evil, know how to give good gifts to your children, how much more will the heavenly Father give the Holy Spirit to those who ask him!" (Luke 11:10–13)

The Word

Concerning the Proclamation of the Church

First, the holy Christian people are recognized by their possession of the holy word of God. To be sure, not all have it in
equal measure, as St. Paul says [1 Cor 3:12.–14]. Some possess
the word in its complete purity, others do not. Those who have
the pure word are called those who "build on the foundation
with gold, silver, and precious stones"; those who do not have
it in its purity are the ones who "build on the foundation with
wood, hay, and straw," and yet will be saved through fire . . .
This is the principal item, and the holiest of holy possessions, by
reason of which the Christian people are called holy; for God's
word is holy and sanctifies everything it touches; it is indeed
the very holiness of God, Romans 1 [:16], "It is the power of
God for salvation to everyone who has faith." [. . .] But we are
speaking of the external word, preached orally by men like you
and me, for this is what Christ left behind as an external sign,
by which his church or his Christian people in the world should
be recognized. [. . .] Now, wherever you hear or see this word
preached, believed, professed, and lived, do not doubt that the
true *ecclesia sancta catholica*, "a Christian holy people," must be

there even though their number is very small. For God's word "shall not return empty," Isaiah 55 [:11], but must have at least a fourth or a fraction of the field. And even if there were no other sign than this alone, it would still suffice to prove that a Christian, holy people must exist there, for God's word cannot be without God's people, and conversely, God's people cannot be without God's word. Otherwise, who would preach or hear it preached, if there were no people of God? And what could or would God's people believe, if there were no word of God?[1]

Once Upon a Time . . .

In order to understand the church's task to proclaim God's Word, we need to understand something about the role narratives play in our common lives. All cultures, societies, and religions have some form of an overarching story or metanarrative that explains and describes existence. This may be more or less distinct, but it provides a framework and gives direction to human striving on both the collective and individual levels. It touches upon the most fundamental questions concerning who we are and why we exist, why things are the way they are, how they ought to really be, and how they can be put right. Very simply, this metanarrative is a central idea concerning the goal of existence and the meaning of life. This narrative constitutes the lens through which we interpret, value, and understand existence. The postmodern era is defined by the collapse of the great narratives, which have been replaced by many different alternatives and competing narratives, each with its own version of what the good life is and how it can be realized. To a large degree, even today's church has lost the great narrative that it participates in. The church's narrative is the biblical history of salvation: the story of creation, fall, covenant, redemption, and the final and total renewal of all things. It is a story where the Triune God and his dealing with the world is central. The biblical narrative of salvation is challenged today by stories that to a large degree revolve around the individual's personal needs, dreams, and demands.

We Must Tell and Retell Our Story

The most serious threat against the great biblical narrative is not only the powers that are trying to distort it, but that, to a large degree, the church has quit retelling it. Storytelling is not only an art to refine, it is the most important commission the church has to administer. Being rooted in a great and common narrative shapes our identity and helps us to understand the world and ourselves. Also, for societies in general, it is of great significance to gather around historically anchoring narratives. Here, we can mention the historical account of the Holocaust and the terrible atrocities that happened in the Nazi era. Today, there are powers that want to revise and eventually wipe out this historical memory. Such a historical revision does not happen overnight, but such a development can occur over several generations. Against this background, initiatives have been taken at different levels to remind us about what really happened during the Nazi era. We are admonished. We must speak about this, telling and retelling the story. For this reason, people arrange seminars and hold days of remembrance with the point being to repeat the story over and over again. If the story is not told, then it is forgotten and replaced by alternatives and false explanations of what happened during these dark decades in Europe.

God's people have always been a storytelling community. We are a people who are called to "proclaim God's powerful deeds" (1 Pet. 2:9).

God has revealed himself in certain events and actions within history. Since the very beginning, he has spoken through his chosen servants and prophets. Yet, in repeating the accounts of this history, we are partakers of God's story concerning the origin and center of existence and its deepest meaning and highest goal. He chooses his people in history; it is this account about God as their God that shapes Israel's identity. It was God who freed them from slavery in Egypt and brought them out on the pilgrimage to the Promised Land. He is the one who offers them hope and a future. Israel is admonished to constantly repeat and inculcate this narrative through speaking, by celebrating holy events and commemorating holidays.

> Hear, O Israel: The LORD our God, the LORD is one. You shall love the LORD your God with all your heart and with all your soul and with all your might. And these words that I command you today shall be on your heart. You shall teach them diligently to your children, and shall talk of them when you sit in your house, and when you walk by the way, and when you lie down, and when you rise. You shall bind them as a sign on your hand, and they shall be as frontlets between your eyes. You shall write them on the doorposts of your house and on your gates (Deut. 6:4–9).

We have also been included in this account because it has culminated in God's saving act through Jesus Christ. The Word dwelt among us and became flesh as the living Word, Jesus Christ. The story of Jesus, his life, death, and resurrection, ascension and return in glory constitutes the epicenter of the biblical narrative. Here, we must think both forward and backward. It is not only that the biblical story lacks focus if it is not understood in light of the cross and the resurrection, it must also be understood backwards, against the background of the great biblical narrative of creation and the fall. It is with such an understanding of the biblical narrative that the mystery of redemption and the foolishness of the cross become good news and God's power of salvation for us. But when the church neglects the biblical story of creation and the fall, the story of Jesus risks being turned into a moralistic improvement program which puts Jesus forth as a role model rather than as a savior. The story about Jesus is then only a series of inspirational tales that try to motivate men to save themselves through their own heroic actions.

Self-help books take up a lot of shelf space in bookstores and perpetually present new techniques for the achievement of happiness and meaning in life. The constant development of different and supposedly better techniques and methods is also an indication that we need something more than good advice. For if self-help techniques had worked, we ought to be helped by now. But there are no techniques, keys, or principles that can help us when it comes to our deepest dilemma as human beings. Only the gospel of Jesus Christ can help with that. When the joyous message concerning what Jesus has done for us is no longer heard in the church and is replaced instead with moralizing appeals, "biblified" life hacks, or banal platitudes telling us how we can have "our best life now," people remain hopeless. Let us hear what the apostle Paul has to say concerning the message that should be heard in the church:

> Let the word of Christ dwell in you richly, teaching and admonishing one another in all wisdom, singing psalms and hymns

and spiritual songs, with thankfulness in your hearts to God (Col. 3:16).

These words imply that if we are not constantly rooted in and reminded of the great biblical narratives because we do not constantly proclaim and retell them, we risk being led by powers other than the Holy Spirit. This also happens in many Christian contexts today. If a person really wants to know what a church believes in, sadly, it is not enough to read references from confessional documents on their website. Instead, a person should pay attention to how they worship. Which story is it that takes shape? Which message is it that is proclaimed? What hope is put forward? What gift is it that is handed out? These are the types of questions that can help us to see what really takes place apart from formal confessions, what is being preached and transferred to the congregation. The historical and common Christian liturgy has been formed precisely for this reason, so that the great story and the gospel message should not be lost but proclaimed through all that is said and done in the church's worship service. This is so Christ's word will dwell richly among us in song, prayer and confession, readings, texts, rites, and actions. When the whole divine service is celebrated as it should be, the great story takes shape, reveals and gives God's great gifts, proclaims and edifies, reminds and roots us in the gospel. Quite simply, it is hard to escape God's Word in a liturgically rich worship service. Different church traditions could stand to test themselves in regard to this statement.

The Reformation and the Return
to the Center of the Story

God's Word was the formal principle for the reformers of the sixteenth century. That is to say, Scripture was the highest authority for doctrine and life and that which should shape the life and worship of the church. According to the reformers, the Word had created the church, and not the other way around. The Augsburg Confession begins by firmly fixing "God's pure word" as the basis upon which all confession and proclamation should rest:

> Accordingly . . . we submit in this case concerning religion our preachers' and our own confession of the manner in which up until now they have taught this doctrine among us based on the Holy Scriptures and the pure word of God.[2]

For Luther, the Bible was the book above all others. He was professor of Biblical Studies in Wittenberg, and as an exegete, he had studied and lectured on many different books of the Bible. He even translated the entire Bible from the original languages into German. Luther's so-called reformational discovery—*justification by faith alone*—was a result of an intensive study of the Bible. Yet, it is important to understand that the reformers were not ivory tower academics. Above all, they were men who tended to and cared for souls as congregational shepherds. They were careful not to treat the Scriptures merely as some sort of Christian history of ideas, but they emphasized how it should be used for the comfort and help of people in worship, proclamation, and the pastoral care of souls. When Luther speaks concerning Scripture, he emphasizes that above all it has a primary function as a means of grace; it is not to be used as a book in which to find sound bites of good advice. The preached Word is not only a speech *about* Christ, but a direct address *from* Christ. He is the Living Word that comes to us and gives us his good gifts through the proclamation of the Word. So, for Luther, Christ is "the kernel and star of Scripture."

The Reformation reestablished the central place of the sermon in the mass and worship. It can be said without exaggeration that the Reformation was a rebirth of preaching. A shift of emphasis occurred so that the saving message that is the central message of the Bible became the focus. Thus, the Reformation was not only concerned with studies about what the Bible says about this and that, but it was also concerned with what the Word accomplishes when it is preached. Luther compared the proclamation of the Word to the creative act of God in the beginning when he spoke light into existence in the midst of darkness. So, the emphasis ended up being that the Word should be proclaimed as an intervening and salvific Word that created life and light. God's Word is living and active, and so a more fitting name for the first mark of the church is *the preached Word* (2 Tim. 4:1–5). So it is not the word as a thing, the "Bible" as a book with diverse and abstract ideas, but the proclamation of the Word as a verb that accomplishes what is preached. God's Word does what it says and says what it does. For this reason, the reformers conceived of the pastoral office above all as a preaching office, and they called it *verbi divini minister* (servants of the divine word). The preacher is not commissioned to present his own views mastering the Word, but to be an obedient servant letting the Word master him and bringing the Word to men as a means of grace for salvation and renewal. In the words of Luther: "To preach the gospel is nothing other than to let Christ come to us."[3]

Carl Axel Aurelius, one of the foremost Luther scholars of our day, vividly describes the centrality of the Divine Service of the Reformation in his book, *Hjärtpunkten* (The Heart of the Faith—the use of the gospel as the key to The Augsburg Confession):

> If the Word is not proclaimed, or if it is only used to describe an event in the past, nothing is distributed. The Word is a promise and a gift, addressed to the gathered congregation. Hence Luther puts stress on the "pronouns":—"Given for you, for the forgiveness of sin"—"Given for you"—"Shed for you."
>
> . . . In the divine service there is meeting between God and man so that the covenant is established, kept and fostered . . . Luther speaks about that which happens between God and the congregation in this encounter as a "joyous exchange." Christ gives that which is his in exchange for that which is ours. This is the liturgy in the literal sense. The conversation in the divine service is between two parties, the present Christ and his people. It is shaped as address and response. It is the living word that stands in the forefront, it wants to say that which shall be heard in the readings and the sermon . . . The service becomes, as Regin Prenter says, "justification in practice."
>
> . . . Such a view of the sermon must result in that the proclamation is given an essential place in the divine service. Among the urgent measures needed for the divine service to regain its original power and clarity, a reestablishment of preaching is necessary. Luther specifies three abuses that harm worship. The first is that to a large degree God's word is despised. The second is that the empty space is filled with empty fables and

legends. The third is that the absence of the Word has caused the divine service to become the work of man trying to assure himself of God's grace and blessing.

. . . The Christian congregation shall never come together (for the divine service) without the preaching of God's word and prayer . . . There are things that must happen in every worship service so that it shall not cease to be the divine service, i.e., a meeting in which the gifts of Christ are distributed and received in faith [that the gospel is proclaimed purely and the sacraments properly administered]. Otherwise, freedom rules. Everything is permissible that furthers the gospel. Nothing is permissible that clouds or contradicts the gospel. That which neither does the one or the other, can be taken or left.[4]

Then this is what God does through the preaching of the Word: he speaks, and through his speech, things come into existence, things that did not exist previously. The light dispels the darkness. Faith is awakened in the heart where unbelief formerly ruled. Order arises out of chaos. Forgiveness is now found where sin once was. The impious are declared righteous. The pulsating life of the Spirit now flows through the new creation where death formerly reigned. *God's Word does what it says and says what it does.* This is why every preacher's task is to set forth Christ and him crucified for us and for the sake of our righteousness. Therefore, preaching is less an explanation and more of a royal announcement, a proclamation of Jesus Christ. We ought to be still and quiet and only listen to the Word through which God deals with us. In preaching, it is God alone who works; we are passive receivers of God's living Word. The Word is thus the form of God's presence among us; it is how God has determined to deal with us. The Word proceeds from his mouth. For this reason, it has power to both kill and make alive. Jesus Christ continues to work through this Word even today. Where his Word goes out, he continues to call disciples, perform miracles, awaken faith, and reveal his glory. For all who listen will hear God's own voice when the text of the Bible is properly expounded and proclaimed. He will speak when the gospel is preached.

But of ourselves, in our fallen condition, we are not interested in the word of the cross that stands at the center of the gospel. If we want to have anything to do with the Bible at all, we would rather keep it as some sort of reference book and not as a means of grace. We would rather source all kinds of principles for success from it, how to be more moral, have a better family life, or speculate concerning revelations and prophecies about the end times. The Bible is certainly full of wisdom that we can apply to life's different circumstances, but as Bo Giertz reminds us: "The Bible shall be read with the intention to learn about salvation . . . Any other use of the Bible is an abuse."[5] To make the Bible into a collection of self-help principles for a successful life is a perversion of its purpose. We then throw the biblical word into the flood of human thoughts that encounter us in diverse religions, philosophies, and popular psychology. As we read the Bible, it can certainly give a common wisdom and advice, but this is not the Bible's essential intention and address.

So, preaching is not about teaching principles for life from the Bible, but about mediating the stream of abundant life that flows from God himself through the Holy Spirit in the Word. Again, Giertz observed, "All that the church does is based on the firm faith that the Word is efficient and that without the Word there is no salvation for this suffering world . . . If the Word does not have any effect on her nothing else will help."[6] A preacher can gather great crowds and even get impressive results if he preaches something that has a natural attraction on the old man instead of the gospel. But the consequences are dire, and he runs the great risk of making God his enemy when he directs man's hope to something other than Christ. We will let Luther summarize these thoughts.

> One thing, and only one thing is necessary for Christian life, righteousness and freedom. That one thing is the most holy Word of God, the gospel of Christ . . . Let us then consider it certain and firmly established that the soul can do without anything except the word of God and that where the word of God is missing there is no help at all for the soul. If it has the Word of God it is rich and lacks nothing since it is the Word of life, truth, light, [. . .] Nor was Christ sent into the world for any other ministry except that of the Word. Moreover, the entire spiritual estate—all the apostles, bishops, and priests—has been called and instituted only for the ministry of the Word.[7]

How Shall We Then Speak about This?

The proclamation of the Word, which is the first and foremost mark of the church, needs to be reestablished among us. The church survives on neither pep talks nor poetry, neither anecdotes nor contemporary contemplations. Conventional entertainment may never take the place of spiritual edification. The Christian proclamation is not explanation but a mediation of Christ and all his blessings for us. Therefore, the preacher's task is to preach God's Word, not to present something that draws people or that men think is interesting to hear. To say it in more biblical terms: the task of proclamation is to feed sheep, not to entertain goats. People wish to have all kinds of random stuff in the divine service if they get to decide themselves, they want to have the spectacular signs, wisdom, and entertainment: "The Jews demand signs and the Greeks wisdom" (1 Cor. 1:22). Together with Paul, the pastor and preacher must therefore say: "But we preach Christ crucified, a stumbling block to Jews and folly to Gentiles, but to those who are called, both Jews and Greeks, Christ the power of God and the wisdom of God" (1 Cor. 1:23–24).

A constant fight continues concerning the great narrative. First and foremost, this fight concerns the center: the gospel. As long as the church has existed, there have been powers, both within and outside the church, that want to pervert the gospel. This fight began in the New Testament times. The most obvious example of this is the situation which arose among the congregations in Galatia. Some passages in Paul's letter to the Galatians can shed light on this:

> I am astonished that you are so quickly deserting him who called you in the grace of Christ and are turning to a different gospel—not that there is another one, but there are some who trouble you and want to distort the gospel of Christ. But even if we or an angel from heaven should preach to you a gospel contrary to the one we preached to you, let him be accursed (Gal. 1:6–8).

> Yet because of false brothers secretly brought in—who slipped in to spy out our freedom that we have in Christ Jesus, so that they might bring us into slavery—to them we did not yield in

submission even for a moment, so that the truth of the gospel might be preserved for you (Gal. 2:4–5).

But when I saw that their conduct was not in step with the truth of the gospel, I said . . . (Gal. 2:14).

[Y]et we know that a person is not justified by works of the law but through faith in Jesus Christ, so we also have believed in Christ Jesus, in order to be justified by faith in Christ and not by works of the law, because by works of the law no one will be justified (Gal. 2:16).

O foolish Galatians! Who has bewitched you? It was before your eyes that Jesus Christ was publicly portrayed as crucified. Let me ask you only this: Did you receive the Spirit by works of the law or by hearing with faith? Are you so foolish? Having begun by the Spirit, are you now being perfected by the flesh? (Gal. 3:1–3).

You are severed from Christ, you who would be justified by the law; you have fallen away from grace (Gal. 5:4).

The same tendencies Paul observed in Galatia were observed by Luther in the church of his day. During the late Middle Ages, the gospel had been somewhat clouded in the church. Through innumerable superstructures and additions, the glory of the gospel had often been overshadowed and obscured by something else. Indulgences, masses, penance, and self-improvement were just some of what was put before men seeking the forgiveness of sins. Certainly, one still spoke about Jesus and his sacrifice but not as sufficient for our salvation and blessedness. The work of Jesus was set forth as a good beginning that must then be completed by diverse religious activities. Blessedness and righteousness did not flow from the completed work of Christ alone, but were to be complemented with man's good works and the merits of the saints. It was a message that did not focus on what God has done for man in Christ, but about what man must do for God. This type of proclamation presented a god who could not be reconciled to us, who would not be completely satisfied by Christ's sacrifice for us and in our stead. Something more must be done. This message, then as now, gives neither peace nor joy, nor thankfulness either, but only uncertainty, angst, and thoughts of damnation—at least, if one takes it seriously and seeks salvation through it. The Reformation's deepest questions germinated in this soil: how can the "monster of incertitude" be conquered? Where can I find a gracious God? How can a sinful man be declared righteous before God?

This distorting of the gospel of grace is then not unique to the sixteenth century. Even today, we wrestle with the same basic questions, even if they are formulated in a different manner. Unfortunately, the pure gospel of Christ and him crucified for us—sufficient for our salvation—is still the church's best-kept secret. Other messages have occupied the central place of the gospel in proclamation and faith. Certainly, there is talk of Jesus, but what is actually said about him? How is he portrayed? What is it he has to offer us sinful men? What kinds of problems does he resolve? How is man's deepest need described? A message that points to sin and guilt has never been a best seller, so it is not so strange that many would rather speak about strategies for life improvement and ways to create a fulfilling life. But to give men a dose of superficial encouragement that is not grounded in the work of the cross and the good news of the gospel is not a part of the Bible's great salvific narrative. To give tips and keys concerning how we can navigate and resolve the puzzles of life can perhaps be seen as valuable, but the point of departure for this message is a narrative different from the biblical story of salvation. Sermons concerning how a man can think bigger, activate his dreams, and believe in himself, are quite simply not addresses from God. The gospel is neither about trying to be kind nor releasing our intrinsic potential as human beings. Moral pointers and campaigns for justice, law, and order, to do for others what you would like others do to you, and so on, are both good and laudable, but they are *not* the gospel's message.

Law and Gospel

How can we then get it right if we want to preach the gospel purely? The reformers saw two distinct addresses in Scripture that are of great help if we want to understand and preach the message of the Bible, namely, *law* and *gospel*. These two words permeate the whole instruction of the Bible. This does not mean making a sharp division between the Old and New Testaments, placing the law in the old and the gospel in the new; there is law in the New Testament, and there is gospel in the Old Testament. On a basic level, we need to understand that law and gospel are two messages that may not be mixed. Mixing has different consequences, but it always happens at the expense of the gospel. When law and gospel are blended, we learn that our salvation depends on our obedience and our deeds. We have then created a message where the work of Jesus is certainly important, even foundational, but which must be completed by our obedience in order to lead to salvation. Salvation is no longer by *grace alone* but a sort of collaborative project where God and man meet halfway. In order to understand why these words cannot be mixed together, we need to pay attention to the entirely different contents of each. The law is a word that simply demands and condemns without mercy if we do not do what it commands. The gospel, on the other hand, is a message that promises us salvation and blessings, free and for nothing. Today, the church tends to play primarily on the law's half-court: "Do this and you can be successful! Do this and you will find peace! Do more and you will be blessed!" The reformers had observed this type of Christianity as purely and simply a religion of the law, even if it is spiced with words of grace and salvation.

However, the confusion of law and gospel suits the old man remarkably. It can really sound quite sensible and fair, perhaps even a bit like wisdom. It is a message consistent with how we gladly look at life: God blesses those who deserve it; God recognizes those who are good and pious; God helps those who help themselves. We come with our sacrifices and gifts for God, and if they please him, then he opens heaven for us. If the prayer is strong enough, if our praise and worship is dedicated enough, and if our discipleship is radical and uncompromising enough, then spiritual breakthrough will come. However, this is not good news for those who know their own sin and weakness. On the contrary, it is really bad news. But those who imagine themselves to be strong can initially feel motivated by the demands to do more, try harder, and go further. Still, it is not the gospel that is heard; it is the message of the law that simply offers a righteousness dependent upon keeping the whole law for the whole time with all of one's heart. Then it is not only an external observation, but even with one's deepest will and motives. It is a righteousness that does not come as a gift from God, but we produce it. It is a righteousness that is not counted to us for Christ's sake, but is given on the basis of one's own merits. But no one experiences peace and righteousness under the law; the law only gives insight concerning what is still lacking, the realization that our sin is much worse, and therefore leads to damnation.

The distinction between law and gospel is occasionally misunderstood when a person supposes that it means ignoring the law and simply preaching grace. The commission of the church is not to abolish the law for the benefit of the gospel. We need to preach both law and gospel, but *without confusion*. When the law is allowed to do its work within us, it plows up the hard crusty soil of the heart and prepares it to receive the good seed of the gospel. Through the law, a person learns to recognize sin and the need for grace and forgiveness. Through the gospel, a person learns to know grace such as it really is, with no "ifs, ands, or buts." The law says: "Do!" The gospel says: "Done!" The law points to the disease, the gospel to the cure. The hard and self-righteous man needs to hear the law. But he who is already weighed down by guilt and is conscious of his insufficiency before God needs to hear the gospel. Now let us take a closer look at the law and gospel in action.

The Task of the Law

Now we know that whatever the law says it speaks to those who are under the law, so that every mouth may be stopped, and the whole world may be held accountable to God. For by works of the law no human being will be justified in his sight, since through the law comes knowledge of sin (Rom. 3:19–20).

In all times, men have been occupied with seeking their own righteousness. They want to appear righteous before God on their own by walking the path of law and works. We all know the law quite well, it characterizes our nature, and therefore also our culture. So the law is not foreign message to us, we know what is right and good and what is wrong and evil. It is written on our hearts, and our conscience constantly reminds us. However, God strengthens the law by giving us his commandments. On a foundational level, God's law reveals his good will for his creation. The law describes what the really good life looks like and how we ought to live in order to be good and fully human. For the most part, it even sounds quite reasonable and rational to all men, especially the second table of the law that deals with how we should interact with our neighbors. Yet, if we are honest, we must admit that we often do not live according to these commandments, even if we believe they are good. The first table, where our relationship to God is regulated, reminds everyone that they do not love God, but in actual fact despise him. Therefore, God's Word makes everyone a sinner, even the moralist who can urge certain commandments and statutes, but in his heart despises God. When we come closer to the law and wrestle with it, we really notice that we have neither the desire nor the will to live as we ought. We even lack the ability to do so. Perhaps from time to time we want to, but even then, we do not do what the law says. Luther's words are telling:

> Although the commandments teach things that are good, the things taught are not done as soon as they are taught, for the commandments show us what we ought to do but do not give us the power to do it. They are intended to teach man to know himself, that through them he may recognize his inability to do good and may despair of his own ability. [. . .] Now when a

man has learned through the commandments to recognize his helplessness and is distressed about how he might satisfy the law—since the law must be fulfilled so that not a jot or tittle shall be lost, otherwise man will be condemned without hope— then, being truly humbled and reduced to nothing in his own eyes, he finds in himself nothing whereby he may be justified and saved.[8]

Thus, the law never makes sinners better; it only makes the sin greater because it unmercifully reveals what our condition is. God's law demands that I am completely holy even as God is holy (Lev. 19:2). Therefore, God's law recognizes nothing but perfection as good. Jesus also demands this when he intensifies the word of the law in the Sermon on the Mount (Matt. 5:48). In certain ways, a person can literally keep the letter of the law, but he lacks its spirit and real intention. Then, a person does what the law demands unwillingly, without heart. A person reluctantly and unwillingly does what is good for fear of punishment or in the hope of reward. When, in this way, a person keeps the law externally, the law reveals how far down the corruption of sin goes within us. It is this that Jesus is after when he intensifies the commandments of the law. If the law only applies externally, then it would be fulfilled if we did the deeds it enjoins and abstained from the deeds it forbids. Yet the law then encompasses man's whole being and directs itself above all at his heart, the very core of where our deepest desires dwell.

If our good deeds are only carried out from fear of punishment and with hope of a reward, then it is done only out of love for ourselves, not for God or our neighbors. If the law did not exist and thus we did not need to fear punishment, we could gladly commit adultery and steal and do all sorts of things that we secretly long to do. This shows that, in the deepest recesses of our hearts, we are really hostile to God's law and, with that, to God himself, regardless of how externally moral we may seem to be. Like someone who simply marries for money, but does not cherish or love his or her partner, we use God as a means to achieve our goals. We turn God into our sugar daddy. We really do not want to have anything to do with him; we only want his stuff and to enjoy his wealth, privileges, and protection. So, no one can be righteous through works of the law. This path is closed (Rom. 3:20).

He who still attempts to go this way only multiplies his sin and heaps sin upon sin, drawing God's judgment upon himself. In this way, the law drives man to hopelessness before God's impossible demand and reveals the sinful depravity of the heart. The gospel will not really be good news for us until God's law has revealed this brutal insight concerning the serious reality of our sin.

The Gospel of God's Grace—the Church's Best-kept Secret

> For I am not ashamed of the gospel, for it is the power of God for salvation to everyone who believes, to the Jew first and also to the Greek. For in it the righteousness of God is revealed from faith for faith, as it is written, "The righteous shall live by faith" (Rom. 1:16–17).

It is then revealed that no one is deemed righteous before God by his own actions and deeds. But how then can God declare someone righteous if no righteous man exists? It is precisely against this background that the gospel becomes really good news. The gospel actually reveals a righteousness that comes from God, thus a righteousness that does not have anything to do with us and our deeds. Only when the light of the law has exposed the sinful depravity within us, shown everything concerning us that is reluctant and rebels against the demands of the law, and leaves us without excuse, only then are we ready to hear the gospel's good news concerning Christ our savior. Jesus Christ has taken my place under the law and fulfilled every jot and tittle of it on my behalf. And not only that, he has also taken my place under the curse of the law, and of his own free will, he has taken our punishment and suffered God's holy judgment in our place. Everything that is mine—sin and unrighteousness—was accounted to him, and everything that is his—righteousness and holiness—was imputed to me. Let us hear how Paul proclaims this good news:

All this is from God, who through Christ reconciled us to himself and gave us the ministry of reconciliation; that is, in Christ God was reconciling the world to himself, not counting their trespasses against them, and entrusting to us the message of reconciliation. Therefore, we are ambassadors for Christ, God making his appeal through us. We implore you on behalf of Christ, be reconciled to God. For our sake he made him to be sin who knew no sin, so that in him we might become the righteousness of God (2 Cor. 5:18–21).

It is precisely here that the grace of the gospel shines the brightest when we understand what *imputed righteousness* really means. The promise of the gospel offers me, weighed down by sin and convinced of my own unworthiness before God, the forgiveness of sins and a perfect righteousness that does not come from myself. This rests simply on

God's mercy and grace through Christ's work for me. When I believe this, it is imputed to me as righteousness. Thus, I have no righteousness of my own to point to, no merits of my own to show, but through faith I am united with Christ and all that is his. Here, faith should not be understood as a new work that I must perform to be righteous through Christ. Faith is the empty hand that has nothing to give; it only receives the gift from God, without anything of my own to contribute. Because this is all about a gift of pure grace in the form of a declaration, it quite simply cannot be received by anything other than faith. To be saved by grace alone is therefore the same as being saved through faith alone in Christ alone. So, the apostle Paul writes here:

> For if Abraham was justified by works, he has something to boast about, but not before God. For what does the Scripture say? "Abraham believed God, and it was counted to him as righteousness." Now to the one who works, his wages are not counted as a gift but as his due. And to the one who does not work but believes in him who justifies the ungodly, his faith is counted as righteousness (Rom. 4:2–5).

> But the words "it was counted to him" were not written for his sake alone, but for ours also. It will be counted to us who believe in him who raised from the dead Jesus our Lord, who was delivered up for our trespasses and raised for our justification. Therefore, since we have been justified by faith, we have peace with God through our Lord Jesus Christ (Rom. 4:23–5:1).

Original sin does not consist in any particular immoral action. It is unbelief, thus mistrust of God, the dishonor of making God into a liar—that is the center of original sin. Fallen man cannot of himself trust in God; it is the Spirit through the proclamation of the gospel that creates faith in the heart (Rom. 10:17). So, even faith is a gift of pure grace. With this faith, we consider God to be trustworthy; we dare to trust in him and the promise he gives us in the gospel. Psychologically speaking, we might consider how a trustworthy person who inspires confidence makes it easy for another to trust his word. He inspires trust and appears worthy of our confidence. We might also think of when we were in love and fell for someone. Our reason cannot exactly explain what happened; we lose control, and love does something with us and in us. It changes us and compels us to cross all natural borders. In a similar way, faith creates faith within us through the proclamation of the gospel. We suddenly find that we believe in the miraculous promise that God places before us. So, the miracle of faith happens in our life. But this is not a one-off event; it is repeated over and over again when the word of the gospel reaches our heart through our ears. In the same way as a marriage is not built upon compulsively holding fast to the early phase of love, but in that one continues to "fall for" each other, so God maintains this faith within us when we place ourselves before his living Word.

Luther himself used the picture of a marriage when he would describe what he called the joyous exchange (*fröhlicher Wechsel*). Christ is the bridegroom whose love compels him to sacrifice himself for the bride, and she reaches out her hand. We are the bride that falls for him and receives his hand. Christ made himself one with the sin of man, and through faith, we become one with Christ's righteousness. All that was ours becomes his; all that was his becomes ours. He took our uneasiness and angst; we receive his peace. We no longer belong to sin, but we are one with Christ. This wonderful word of Luther is worth citing:

> The third incomparable benefit of faith is that it unites the soul with Christ as a bride is united with her bridegroom. By the mystery as the Apostle teaches, Christ and the soul become one flesh [Eph. 5:31–32]. And if they are one flesh . . . it follows that everything they have they hold in common, the good as well as the evil. Accordingly, the believing soul can boast of and glory in whatever Christ has as though it were its own and whatever the soul has Christ claims as his own. Let us compare these and we shall see inestimable benefits. Christ is full of grace, life, and salvation. The soul is full of sins, death and damnation. Now let faith come between them and sins, death, and damnation will be Christ's, while grace, life and salvation will be the soul's. [. . .] Here we have a most pleasing vision . . . Christ is God and man in one person. He has neither sinned nor died, and is not condemned and he cannot sin, die, or be condemned; his righteousness, life and salvation are unconquerable, eternal, omnipotent. By the wedding ring of faith he shares in the sins, death, and pains of hell which are his bride's. As a matter of fact, he makes them his own and acts as if they were his own and as if he himself had sinned; he suffered, died and descended into hell that he might overcome them all. Now since it was such a one who did all this, and death and hell could not swallow him up, these were necessarily swallowed up by him in a mighty duel; for his righteousness is greater than the sins of all men, his life stronger than death, his salvation more invincible than

hell. Thus the believing soul by means of the pledge of its faith is free in Christ, its bridegroom, free from all sins, secure against death and hell, and is endowed with the eternal righteousness, life, and salvation of Christ, its bridegroom. [. . .] Who then can fully appreciate what this royal marriage means? Who can understand the riches of the glory of his grace? Here this rich and divine bridegroom Christ marries this poor, wicked harlot, redeems her from all her evil, and adorns her with all his goodness. Her sins cannot now destroy her, since they are laid upon Christ and swallowed up by him. And she has that righteousness in Christ her husband, of which she may boast as of her own and which she can confidently display alongside her sins in the face of death and say, "If I have sinned, yet my Christ, in whom I believe, has not sinned, and all his is mine and all mine is his."[9]

Through faith, we have thus been declared righteous, and so we have peace with God (Rom. 5:1). The sign of this is that God gives us his Holy Spirit, who gives birth to new life in us. This life of the Spirit now flows with desire and power to live in accordance with God's will, not only literally, according to external works, but with its deepest contents. This is the gospel, the good news concerning the righteousness that offers us grace alone through faith alone in Christ alone. It is this gift that is offered to us in God's Word and is mediated to us through the means of grace that are the gospel's pure proclamation and the proper administration of the sacraments.

CHAPTER 5

Baptism

Concerning the Church's Bath of Grace

Second, God's people or the Christian holy people are recognized by the holy sacrament of baptism, wherever it is taught, believed, and administered correctly according to Christ's ordinance. That too is a public sign and a precious, holy possession by which God's people are sanctified. It is the holy bath of regeneration through the Holy Spirit [Titus 3:5], in which we bathe and with which we are washed of sin and death by the Holy Spirit, as in the innocent holy blood of the Lamb of God. Wherever you see this sign you may know that the church, or the holy Christian people, must surely be present . . . Indeed you should not pay attention to who baptizes, for baptism does not belong to the baptizer, nor is it given to him, but it belongs to the baptized. It was ordained for him by God, and given to him by God, just as the word of God is not the preacher's (except in so far as he too hears and believes it) but belongs to the disciple who hears and believes it; to him is it given.[1]

Baptism—Union with Christ and His Body

The church took form during a great celebration of baptism. In this way, people were urged to receive the forgiveness of sins at the first Pentecost: through faith, conversion, and baptism. Baptism then marks the entrance into the Christian life, whereby we take part in the Christian church. "So those who received his word were baptized, and there were added that day about three thousand souls. And they devoted themselves to the apostles' teaching and the fellowship, to the breaking of bread and the prayers" (Acts 2:41–42). A person can observe baptism as the entrance of the church and the new life in Christ in physical form when entering old historical churches. The first thing to be observed within the doors of the church is the baptismal font. By its mere presence and position, it proclaims that it does not do to enter the church without passing through the waters of baptism. The location of the baptismal font also becomes a wonderful reminder for those who are already baptized. As a first address given even before the divine service starts, the message that is communicated says: I am baptized, my old man is dead and buried with Christ, the life I now live is the new life in Christ through God's grace. So, baptism has defined the church since her earliest days. Even today, baptism is the most important ecumenical sign in the worldwide Christian church. We confess baptism as a sacrament in the ecumenical creeds "for the remission of sins." Even if there are different baptismal practices, most traditions agree that a Christian baptism is valid before God, and the baptisms of other traditions are increasingly given mutual recognition. The requirements for the validity of a baptism to be recognized is that it happened in water at Christ's command in the name of the Father, the Son, and the Holy Spirit. The World Council of Churches says the following about baptism in the BEM-Document (Baptism, Eucharist, and Ministry): "Baptism is an action that cannot be repeated. Every practice that can be interpreted as 'rebaptism' must be avoided . . . Mutual recognition of baptism is commonly considered as an important sign and means of expressing the baptismal unity given in Christ. Everywhere that it is possible mutual recognition ought to be expressly spoken of by the churches."[2]

We are united through baptism not only with Christ, but with all his body—the church—in all times. We are thus united in Christ across all borders; neither time nor space, ethnicity, gender nor class are any longer markers of our deepest identity: "For in Christ Jesus you are all sons of God, through faith. For as many of you as were baptized into Christ have put on Christ. There is neither Jew nor Greek, there is neither slave nor free, there is no male and female, for you are all one in Christ Jesus" (Gal. 3:26–28). Therefore baptism has a very fundamental meaning for Christian unity, and we are admonished to work for its full realization. As Paul expresses it:

> I therefore, a prisoner for the Lord, urge you to walk in a manner worthy of the calling to which you have been called, with all humility and gentleness, with patience, bearing with one another in love, eager to maintain the unity of the Spirit in the bond of peace. There is one body and one Spirit—just as you were called to the one hope that belongs to your call—one Lord, one faith, one baptism, one God and Father of all, who is over all and through all and in all (Eph. 4:1–6).

The Deformation and Reformation of Baptism

Our theology and practice around baptism may need reforming. All the baptized need to discover what they possess in baptism, and local congregations need to consider their members in light of baptism's wonderful reality. Despite baptism's relatively simple configuration, it has a very deep meaning and carries with it enormous wealth. So, baptism should not be reduced to a festive name-giving ceremony, and an occasion for family and relatives to meet under festive circumstances. In baptism, we celebrate life from a perspective greater than that of creation; above all, we celebrate new life from the perspective of salvation, the new creation in Christ (2 Cor 5:17). Yet, it is also possible to end up in the opposite extreme where a person is so concerned with the seriousness of baptism that severe qualifications are considered necessary. With such a view of baptism, it becomes a sort of diploma for "worthy" Christians who have fulfilled criteria for knowledge and maturity in faith.

Neither can baptism be privatized or characterized by the zeitgeist's individualistic powers. It belongs at home in the public worship of the local congregation, as an expression of Christ's church, because baptism is an incorporation into the body of Christ, and the one who is baptized becomes a part of the congregation's communion. Good instruction about baptism is also needed, not only concerning the act of baptism but also the gift, comfort, and assurance that the baptized possess in their baptism for the rest of their lives. In worship and proclamation, the church needs to regularly link baptism and its foundational meaning to the whole of Christian life. It may not be reduced to a first step on the path of many following steps toward spiritual development. It cannot be emphasized enough that baptism is not based in our individual determination to follow Jesus, but instead in the determination of Jesus to follow, obey, and fulfill the Father's will in our place and for us. With an inaccurate emphasis on our own role in baptism, a person could get the idea that they need to be rebaptized. When the emphasis is laid upon our own efforts and our own determination to follow Jesus, a person might worry about their condition when he or she does not successfully live up to the demands of discipleship. But the good news of baptism is that it does not rest upon our promise to God, but on God's promise to us. Yet, baptism cannot be practiced in an indiscriminate way and become a mark for some kind of human rights, i.e., peace, love, and understanding, regardless of faith in Jesus Christ. Baptism cannot be sufficient for those who neither want nor have the intention of receiving Christ's gift or living in his church. Without this perspective, a person risks eroding the meaning of baptism and obscuring the real gift. It even helps to increase the uncertainty of baptism's validity for the individual. It also makes it harder for other Christian traditions to recognize all baptisms as valid baptisms. Here, different Christian traditions need to take responsibility and see to it that baptism is handled as the holy sacrament that it is.

Why then is baptism so central for the church and for the individual Christian? What does it really mean? What happens in baptism and what does it mean for my everyday life? How does baptism give me comfort and what wealth do I possess in baptism? These and related questions stand at the center of the rest of this chapter.

Let Us Take It from the Beginning

Water has played a central role in the world since the dawn of creation and throughout the whole Old Testament. Water symbolizes a powerful force that can both extinguish and give life. It was from the waters that God called creation forth merely through his word. With water, he drowned the old world and saved Noah. In the Red Sea, the people of Israel received their baptism; through water, he freed them from Egyptian slavery and at the same time drowned their enemies (1 Cor. 10:1–4). With the admonition of the prophet Elijah, Naaman dipped himself seven times in the water and was cured of his leprosy (2 Kings 5:10, 14). Water also makes important appearances in different rites and holy acts that are observed as mediators of God's special touch. We read about different ablutions, washings, and baths in the Old Testament. A spiritual cleansing is carried out through these actions, and even the priests and Levites are consecrated to service in the tabernacle through rites of washing with water. Groups of people who have been excluded from the community for various reasons, for example, lepers, could be once again incorporated into the community through washings of water after a documented healing (Mark 1:40–44). These various examples show that the baptism of the New Testament is foreshadowed in the Old Testament. When Ezekiel, the prophet of the exile, prophesied about the New Covenant, he took up this thread concerning the purifying and sanctifying water: "I will sprinkle clean water on you, and you shall be clean from all your uncleanness, and from all your idols I will cleanse you. And I will give you a new heart, and a new spirit I will put within you. And I will remove the heart of stone from your flesh and give you a heart of flesh. And I will put my Spirit within you and cause you to walk in my statutes and be careful to obey my rules" (Ez. 36:25–27). But as modern men we ask: how can simple water have such power to accomplish all this? It sounds like a superstition or something magic. Here, we might remember Luther's words concerning the waters of baptism:

> Clearly the water does not do it, but the Word of God, which is with and alongside the water, and faith, which trusts this Word of God in the water. For without the Word of God the water is plain water and not a baptism, but with the Word of God it is a baptism, that is, a grace-filled water of life and a "bath of the new birth in the Holy Spirit."[3]

When John the Baptist points to Christ, he describes him as the one who would fulfill the prophecy of Ezekiel that we read above. The Pharisees, who knew the Scriptures, at one point ask the Baptist: "Why do you baptize if you are not the Messiah?" (John 1:25) So they confirm with their question the proposition that the Messiah would baptize the people. John answers them by pointing to Jesus and saying: "Behold, the Lamb of God, who takes away the sin of the world! . . . I myself did not know him, but he who sent me to baptize with water said to me, 'He on whom you see the Spirit descend and remain, this is he who baptizes with the Holy Spirit'" (John 1:29–33). John's baptism was a baptism of repentance that men did for God. It was an outer sign of their desire to repent. But Christian Baptism builds upon and mediates what Christ has done for us. In this baptism, it is God who deals with us, not we who do something for him. In this baptism, he gives precisely what Ezekiel had prophesied: the forgiveness of sins and the Holy Spirit. It is this baptism that the Lord himself has instituted and is central to the great commission: "Go therefore and make disciples of all nations, baptizing them in the name of the Father and of the Son and of the Holy Spirit, teaching them to observe all that I have commanded you. And behold, I am with you always, to the end of the age" (Matt. 28:19–20). This baptism is then carried further by the apostles and mission of the church in the Roman Empire and to the far ends of the earth even up to our day. Yet the baptismal texts in Acts only report what happened; we do not receive any explanation concerning the deeper meaning of baptism. We receive that in the epistolary texts, and particularly in Paul's. Therefore, we cannot build our baptismal theology exclusively on passages from the gospels and Acts. When we do this, we can easily be overly occupied by the order that appears there, first faith and then baptism, which naturally arises from the missional setting. The meaning of baptism becomes central in the rest of the New Testament where nothing is made of the order between faith and baptism.

The Meaning and Work of Baptism

The following are a few questions : we need to ask: does a person really have to be baptized, is faith not enough? If baptism is so important, what then is it that is mediated in baptism? How and when is this then to be done? As I said above, baptism is instituted by Christ himself. Yet it is important to understand that it is not instituted for him but for us. God does just fine without baptism; he can mediate and give his gifts however he wants. But for the sake of our weak faith, he has tied his promise to certain external physical signs and actions, and baptism is one of them. You can always doubt your own faith, but an action and sign that God has instituted stands firm. Thus, it is not actually the action that saves, but God himself through the promise that he tied to baptism. As Luther said:

> But faith is always lacking, since when it comes to faith we
> have enough to learn for an entire lifetime. It can happen that

a person can say "Look, faith was once present but is no longer." But baptism lacks for nothing. No one can say "Look, there was once a baptism, but it is no longer there." Baptism still stands because the institution of God still stands and what has been done according to his institution both stands and will remain.[4]

In a very particular way, baptism portrays the gospel's center—Jesus Christ's death and resurrection—and how God gives us salvation through Christ. It visualizes both what happened to Christ and what happens to us now when we are united with him. In baptism, the old man is killed and buried, so that we are resurrected with Christ to new life. On the cross, Jesus won salvation. This salvation is mediated to us through the preached Word and the sacraments of baptism and the Lord's Supper. It is through these channels that we receive the gifts of God in faith. In an earlier chapter, I called the sacraments God's distribution channels. This means that we are not dealing with mere symbols, but salvation is really mediated to us through these external channels. So, it deals with something much greater than man confirming what he has determined in an external rite. The sacraments do not belong to the law—as something we do for God, but to the gospel—as something God does for us. It is God in Christ who gives us the forgiveness of sins in water, bread, and wine; faith only has to receive this. So, baptism does not add anything to faith, but faith receives help and takes hold of God's promise through a visible sign and a physical action. As Peter proclaimed on the first Pentecost: "Be baptized every one of you in the name of Jesus Christ for the forgiveness of your sins" (Acts 2:38). Bengt Hägglund, a legendary Lutheran theologian from the University of Lund, reasons concerning this: "One can ask how baptism is related to the word because even when the word is received, it speaks, works, regenerates and gives the forgiveness of sins. The difference apparently lies in that the sacrament is bound to an outer element, the water, and thereby becomes a visible sign for the single individual. Baptism also marks more clearly than the word, the actual entrance of the individual into the church's communion and their reception into the congregation."[5] Or, as Luther has so adeptly expressed it in his Large Catechism: "For my faith does not make baptism; rather, it receives baptism."[6]

Let us look a little closer at the words with which we are baptized: "The name of the Father and of the Son and the Holy Spirit." That we are baptized in the Father's name means that we are received as his children in baptism. We are adopted by the Father and are his true children and enter his family (Gal. 3:26–29; Eph. 1:5). That we are baptized in the name of the Son both proclaims and unites us with the death and resurrection of Jesus Christ for the forgiveness of our sins. When we are dipped under the water, the old life is buried, and we die with Christ. When we are lifted up out of the water, a new life begins because we are raised with Christ. This action also pictures a future promise concerning eternal life. One day we shall be buried dead in a grave, but precisely as we are brought low and lifted up from the baptismal grave, so shall we one day rise physically to eternal life. So, through baptism, we receive salvation's gift and the forgiveness of sins through faith. As Paul writes to Titus:

> For we ourselves were once foolish, disobedient, led astray,
> slaves to various passions and pleasures, passing our days
> in malice and envy, hated by others and hating one another.

But when the goodness and loving kindness of God our Savior appeared, he saved us, not because of works done by us in righteousness, but according to his own mercy, by the washing of regeneration and renewal of the Holy Spirit, whom he poured out on us richly through Jesus Christ our Savior, so that being justified by his grace we might become heirs according to the hope of eternal life. The saying is trustworthy, and I want you to insist on these things, so that those who have believed in God may be careful to devote themselves to good works. These things are excellent and profitable for people (Titus 3:3–8).

Baptism in the name of the Son also means a new identity. So, as we are enveloped by water, we are now completely sealed in Christ. "For as many of you as were baptized into Christ have put on Christ" (Gal. 3:27). We live our new life in and through Christ, and Christ in and through us. "To them God chose to make known how great among the Gentiles are the riches of the glory of this mystery, which is Christ in you, the hope of glory" (Col. 1:27).

That we are baptized in the name of the Holy Spirit means that we take part in the Holy Spirit: "Be baptized every one of you in the name of Jesus Christ for the forgiveness of your sins, and you will receive the gift of the Holy Spirit" (Acts 2:38). We are baptized in and united with the whole body of Christ where the Spirit's unity rules: "For in one Spirit we were all baptized into one body—Jews or Greeks, slaves or free—and all were made to drink of one Spirit" (1 Cor. 12:13). So, by the Spirit, we participate in God's own life that sanctifies and works the character of Christ in and through us: "But the fruit of the Spirit is love, joy, peace, patience, kindness, goodness, faithfulness, gentleness, self-control; against such things there is no law" (Gal. 5:22–23). The Spirit make us into channels that mediate God's blessings to bring comfort and edification:

> To each is given the manifestation of the Spirit for the common good. For to one is given through the Spirit the utterance of wisdom, and to another the utterance of knowledge according to the same Spirit, to another faith by the same Spirit, to another gifts of healing by the one Spirit, to another the working of miracles, to another prophecy, to another the ability to distinguish between spirits, to another various kinds of tongues, to another the interpretation of tongues. All these are empowered by one and the same Spirit, who apportions to each one individually as he wills (1 Cor. 12:7–11).

The Validity of Baptism

As pastors, we frequently encounter anxious concerns regarding baptism in the pastoral care of souls. For example, a person can doubt his baptism because it happened under sketchy circumstances. When one is older, he may question his own faith or his earlier understanding of baptism. Perhaps he has not lived in his baptism nor taken part in the divine service for many years. This and similar things can lead a person to question the validity of their own baptism. Yet, here it is important to understand that baptism is something greater than our experiences and circumstances, inclusive of our sins. Baptism is objective, and its validity rests on something that God himself has commanded and done. Just as Christ does not need to die anew for our sins every time we sin, so we do not need to be baptized again when we fall or backslide. From a perspective of soul care (pastoral counseling), it is therefore of the greatest importance that we hold fast to a clear and obvious instruction from Scripture concerning the validity of baptism and that we endeavor for good and proper ordinances concerning how baptism is done. Then there is the presumption that baptism shall be a wonderful comfort and assurance of God's grace as it is thought to be for all baptized. As it is expressed in the *Apology to the Augsburg Confession*,

> We have need of external signs of so great a promise because a conscience full of fear has need of manifold consolation . . . baptism and the Lord's Supper are signs that continually admonish, cheer, and encourage desponding minds to believe more firmly that their sins are forgiven.[7]

It is very sad that in our days there are so many unclear baptisms. Not that it impinges on the validity of baptism, but it obscures the meaning and reality of baptism for the baptized. Sloppy and unclear baptisms also cloud the wealth we possess in this sacrament for the church as a whole. So, every baptism ought to be administered properly within the worshiping congregation. Liturgy and proclamation should take clear form and proclaim the rich and wonderful contents of baptism. It serves as a constant reminder for all those already baptized of what they possess in baptism and is an obvious reference point we can take refuge in during all the storms of life. And let us establish: baptism does not rest on personal memory. None of us doubts that we were born despite the fact that we cannot remember our own birth. So, there is nothing, neither with the administrator of baptism or the baptismal candidate, that can make baptism ineffective or invalid.

Certain things can obscure the meaning of baptism, but nothing can thwart its work. Rebaptism does not cancel the content and essence of baptism, but rather erodes its meaning. Karl Barth expresses this well in his little writing on baptism:

> The paradoxical fact can arise that the church itself does not know what it does with baptism and what it possesses in the baptized, and on their side the baptized do not know that they are baptized or what they possess in the baptism the church has given them. But an objective destruction of the essence of baptism, an objective thwarting of its power, an objective hindrance of its work and thus an objective futility in baptism on the grounds of poor administration and poor reception of the sacrament cannot come into question.[8]

A baptized man differentiates himself through his baptism from an unbaptized person. Through baptism, he is united with Christ's death and resurrection. He lives his life under the name of the triune God and has received the sign of God's saving grace. Whether or not he himself lives in, thinks about, or believes this, he is marked for all time by God's sign. He cannot undo this by leaving the communion of the church or by calling himself an atheist. This gift is given by God and remains for all eternity. But faith and baptism belong together. What God gives in baptism must be received through faith. Without faith, baptism's gifts lie untapped and are of no use to the baptized. But the gift remains there the whole time and waits and wants to be employed and received in faith. Among our people there is a slumbering revival that waits to be resurrected through the proclamation of the gospel. Millions of people in our land have received the gift of baptism, but because of an unclear order and instruction for many people, it is unclear as to what they possess in baptism. The foundational message for us all then is simply: if you are baptized, believe in your baptism and apply the gift that you already have. If you believe but are not baptized, be baptized and receive the riches of baptism. The content of baptism is nothing other than the content of the gospel. However, baptism is a way to receive the gospel physically in faith with the body and not only with the heart. It gives a wonderful comfort and assurance that you are now in Christ and Christ is in you. A person should be careful about making statements with certainty concerning what happens to a person who is not baptized. As was said, baptism was not instituted for God's sake, but for our sake. If it happens for different reasons that a person is not baptized, for instance, in the case of the thief on the cross, then we should know that it is faith that saves. But if we can be baptized, we should do it for our own sake. Let us never forget that baptism is not a demand we should fulfill but a gift to be received.

To Live in Your Baptism

What I have emphasized above is that baptism only happens once and at the beginning of our Christian life, but it is a valid and perpetual reality for the entire future. In baptism, we actually clothed ourselves in Christ, in his death and resurrection. We possess all this already. Simultaneously, this means a lifelong growth in baptism where every day we develop and root ourselves within the contents of baptism. Therefore, briefly said, the Christian life is to live in your baptism, dead to sin and living in and for Christ. So, baptism indicates the actual pattern for our Christian life, the cruciform life, to die and rise with Christ every day. In this also lies the "mystery" of a "victorious"

Christian life—namely, to give up our own control and our perpetual attempts to form our lives according to our own fashion. To give up our own fight and to be enveloped in Christ's victory over sin, death, and Satan, that we already possess in our baptism: "For through the law I died to the law, so that I might live to God. I have been crucified with Christ. It is no longer I who live, but Christ who lives in me. And the life I now live in the flesh I live by faith in the Son of God, who loved me and gave himself for me" (Gal. 2:19–20).

> In baptism, therefore, every Christian has enough to study and practice all his or her life. Christians always have enough to do to believe firmly what baptism promises and brings—victory over death and the devil, forgiveness of sin, God's grace, the entire Christ, and the Holy Spirit with his gifts.[9]

Baptism is therefore invaluable in relation to the daily plague of sin with all the struggles and temptations that meet us in life. Many different powers surround us and threaten us, but we meet them all as baptized Christians. We no longer have any debt towards our sinful demands and need not let them dictate how we live our lives. As Paul says: "So you also must consider yourselves dead to sin and alive to God in Christ Jesus. Let not sin therefore reign in your mortal body, to make you obey its passions. Do not present your members to sin as instruments for unrighteousness, but present yourselves to God as those who have been brought from death to life, and your members to God as instruments for righteousness" (Rom. 6:11–13). A way to remind ourselves of the reality of baptism is to make the sign of the cross upon ourselves. For what is it that we essentially do when we make the sign of the cross? When we make this sign, we cover our whole body with the cross of Christ from head to foot with the baptismal word. The same words were spoken over us when the waters of baptism covered and buried us, when our old life ceased in our death and resurrection with Christ. In the name of the Father and of the Son and of the Holy Spirit. We also frame every worship service with these words. We say them in the invocation, during the absolution, after communion, and conclude with it in connection to the benediction. It is also a good custom to begin and end every day with these words. I prefer to do it myself when I wash my face or take a shower. I remind myself that precisely as water washes over me, I have been purified in the waters of baptism and have received new life in Christ. Baptism envelops the entirety of our life from rebirth to the resurrection. Therefore, in baptism I have already encountered death. So, for the baptized, death does not lie and lurk before us, but it is really behind us. This life I live here and now I live in God's grace as revealed in Jesus Christ. My life no longer belongs to me. That thought originates with original sin. My life belongs to Christ. As Paul says:

> I appeal to you therefore, brothers, by the mercies of God, to present your bodies as a living sacrifice, holy and acceptable to God, which is your spiritual worship. Do not be conformed to this world, but be transformed by the renewal of your mind, that by testing you may discern what is the will of God, what is good and acceptable and perfect (Rom. 12:1–2).

The Lord's Supper

Concerning the Church's Table of Grace

Third, God's people, or Christian holy people, are recognized by the holy sacrament of the altar, wherever it is rightly administered, believed and received, according to Christ's institution. This too is a public sign and a precious, holy possession left behind by Christ by which his people are sanctified so that they also exercise themselves in faith and openly confess that they are Christian, just as they do with the word and with baptism. [. . .] Wherever you see this sacrament properly administered, there you may be assured of the presence of God's people. For as was said above of the word wherever God's word is, there the church must be; likewise, wherever baptism and the sacrament are, God's people must be, and vice versa.[1]

You Are What You Eat

"What should we eat?' This is perhaps the most common question we ask each other. Food and mealtimes are a constant theme of discussion. We eat both to survive and for enjoyment, fun food and bland food. We eat alone, and we eat together. Food is a given ingredient of both everyday community and ceremonial celebration. There is no true midsummer without herring, no Cajun boil without crawdads, and no Thanksgiving without turkey. The meal is a big deal. For many men, food and drink is also a comfort when one feels lonely, and in the Western world, abuse has been a serious health problem. Food is also strongly linked to our striving after looking good and fit. Every day, we hear about different alleged miracle-working diets through newspapers, TV, and social media. So, we have a two-sided relationship to food. It gives us life and strength, community and joy, but it can also be a problem, even leading to an early death. "Man ought to eat lest he die. One eats, and he still dies," as someone has expressed it. The fact is that while parts of the world starve to death, so it is that other parts of the world literally take their lives with the help of the fork and knife. But despite everything, we are dependent on eating and drinking. However, it is not unimportant what we stuff ourselves with. Mood, skin, and heart—everything is affected by what and how we eat. So, one can rightly say that we are what we eat.

If we reflect theologically on the meaning food has for life, then *dependent* and *from without* become two key terms. Man is completely dependent on food that comes to him from without. This relationship between man and food is anchored in God's order; God sustains all of creation and gives life through food. So, food is the means through which God gives life and strength to earthly creatures, who, for this reason, are indirectly yet completely dependent upon him. As the Psalmist so beautifully expressed it: "The eyes of all look to you, and you give them their food in due season. You open your hand; you satisfy the desire of every living thing" (Psalm 145:15–16). Without food, a man can survive as long as fifty or sixty days, and without water, hardly longer than ten days. When the body lacks nourishment, the functions of the body are significantly affected. The body begins to act up and ceases to operate as it should. Finally, all the functions of life cease, and the body shuts down completely.

So it is even with the body of Christ. As God's people, we live by the nourishment that God gives us through the Word and sacraments. They are channels through which God gives us life. When the gospel does not ring out loud and clear, and when the sacraments are not properly administered in the church, malnourishment occurs and life slows down. Then the temptation to quickly solve the problem arises. If we are not anchored in good theology and liturgy, we rely instead on our own solutions to improve our situation. A new conference, exciting speakers with spectacular themes, pop worship, a more "relevant" sermon—the creative proposals are many. If we couple these different solutions to our need to eat, it can be compared to satiating oneself with fast food. It gives us quick carbohydrates and a momentary feeling of satisfaction. Or why not candy? Sugar is sweet, picks us up, and gives an immediate stimulation, a positive effect. But the long-term effects of fast food and candy are not good. Over the long haul, such food is devastating. Yet, this substitute for real food is common in Christendom. We want to have a quick fix and fast results, and we appear willing to try almost anything except receiving the real and nourishing food that God gives us through the Word and sacraments.

We who serve as pastors and leaders have a great responsibility here. In certain respects, our task could be compared to a parent's concern for their children. Out of love for our children, we as parents seek to teach them healthy eating habits early. It seems by nature that children prefer less nourishing food. But taste is not static. It develops over the years, and in time, we learn to like what at first does not taste good. As parents, we know that we cannot defer to the preferences of children when it comes to food. We untiringly continue to put vegetables on the table. In the same way, the church cannot adapt to the personal preferences of people and worldly tastes. The church and her consecrated servants must stubbornly insist on serving the food that really gives life and health. Here, we stand on the words of Jesus himself: "Man shall not live by bread alone" (Matt. 4:4). The spiritual meaning of food is an important theme in the Bible. Eating plays a central role in both the fall and redemption. "But of the tree of the knowledge of good and evil you shall not eat, for in the day that you eat of it you shall surely die" (Gen. 2:17). Man ate of the forbidden fruit and he died. But even the forgiveness of sins and the gift of life is given to us through food, namely, the meal served at our Lord's table: "Take, eat; this is my body" (Matt. 26:26). Jesus Christ has given us his promise that whoever comes to him shall never be hungry or thirst (John 6:35). The food he gives is real food for the spirit, soul, and body (John 6:55). He himself is the bread of life, and whoever eats of this food that he gives shall live even if he dies (John 11:25). This promise of Jesus brings a whole new dimension to the old expression "you are what you eat."

The Lord's Supper: Means, Meaning, and Mystery

How can we then understand the deeper meaning of the Lord's Supper? Why is it so central for the church? What does it mediate and how can we receive this mystery? The Lord's Supper is a gift that the Lord Jesus Christ himself has given to the church. From Scripture and other sources that describe the early church, we can presume that it was celebrated with a high frequency and great joy. The Lord's Supper was one of the signs that characterized the congregational life of the New Testament. Already in the beginning of Acts, we read that "they devoted themselves to the apostles' teaching and the fellowship, to the breaking of bread and the prayers" (Acts 2:42). Considering the central place of the Lord's Supper in the Bible, the early church, and through-out the church's history, there is surprisingly little talk of it in some evangelical circles today. This is partly based on a confused theological understanding of the Lord's Supper. If a person is uncertain about the meaning, a person can understand why it is not celebrated and given a more prominent place. Clearly, the Supper is poor as entertainment if someone has bought into the worldly perspective of what a divine service should be. But the Lord's Supper was not instituted to entertain, but on the contrary to maintain the people of God, and for this purpose, it is essential. The Lord's Supper will never receive stars in the *Michelin Guide*, but for all its simplicity, it smacks of heaven.

The Lord's Supper is not primarily food for the stomach but a "food of the soul, for it nourishes and strengthens the new creature," as Luther expressed it.[2] During the Reformation, it was not only the proclaimed gospel that was emphasized, the Lord's Supper was also given high appraisal. Luther wrote extensively about it and reformed not only the sermon but to comprehensive degree even the sacrament of the altar. In the church life of the late Middle Ages, the Lord's Supper had in large part come to be a spectacle of the Mass. The priest consecrated and consumed the bread and wine, and the people looked on. Through this practice, the meaning of the Mass had become practically distorted, and its character as a means of grace was hidden under all kinds of abuse and unbiblical superstructures. In all ages, it has been necessary to rediscover the rich blessings of the Lord's Supper and declare its true meaning. Allow me to be a little blunt here and cite the legendary pioneer leader of the Swedish Pentecostal movement, Lewi Pethrus. In the series *"Trons Hemlighet,"* a person can read that he "distances himself from both the Roman Catholic doctrine concerning the Lord's Supper, and from the reformed views that arose in the sixteenth century, where the bread and the wine are only seen as external signs. Instead, he joins himself to a view that lies closer to the Lutheran and which also arises from early church's reading of the New Testament texts." In 1912, Pethrus lectured concerning the Lord's Supper and said:

> There are many beloved children of God who have never thought of what it means to sit down and eat the bread and drink the cup. And because they don't understand the meaning, they lose the blessing that they otherwise would receive. For me this truth is like a diamond, like a pearl that sparkles, shines, glitters and steals my soul, and the more I look at it the shinier and more glorious it is.[3]

Thus, Pethrus couples the experience of the Lord's Supper to a clear understanding of its meaning. This is why it is important that pastors and priests instruct concerning the Lord's Supper so that God's people understand what wealth they are being offered. There is then nothing that can so clearly help us to understand the Lord's Supper's meaning and blessing as to diligently and reverently celebrate it as an obvious part of the congregation's ordinary service. When the Lord's Supper is laid aside for a particularly special gathering, outside the regular worship life, the divine service loses its true center where Christ is present and gives himself to us through the bread and wine of the Lord's Supper. Luther emphasizes the importance of familiarizing themselves with the meaning of the Lord's Supper:

> So we must speak about the second sacrament in the same way under three headings, stating what it is, what its benefits are, and who is to receive it. All this is established from the words Christ used to institute it. So everyone who wishes to be a Christian and go to the sacrament should know them.[4]

The Lord's Supper—A Table of Grace

Eating together and asking others to sit at the dinner table was deeply meaningful in antiquity. In the Jewish and biblical milieu in which Jesus lived, meals were strictly regulated because table fellowship had such deep meaning. With whom one ate mattered just as much as what one ate. This can seem foreign to us, but if we think about it then, we can see correlations to this in our day too. Our meals are also marked by certain ritual elements and arrangements. In ceremonial settings, guest lists are often celebrated along with the menu and table placement. Certain measures of wit and etiquette are also important. It is through such arrangements that the meals are given greater importance. However, people do not just come together to eat. There is a point to the meal expressed by various, almost ritualistic elements and arrangements. If we go back to the milieu in which Jesus lived, we notice that several of the controversies in which Jesus found himself played themselves out in and around meals. The critique most often directed at Jesus from the Pharisees and the scribes was not about what was served for food and drink, but about who shared table fellowship with Jesus (Luke 5:30–32; 15:1–2). Jesus broke bread with sinners and included them in his communion. At this time, breaking bread and sharing meals was connected to a kind of covenant. Those who shared table fellowship stood in covenant with each other. They accepted each other. The meal signaled that the communion did not have any barriers and that peace and redemption ruled. In other words, "just" eating and drinking together was never a "just" in this context. It had strong social and religious dimensions.

The evening before Jesus was to be crucified and killed, he instituted a meal that cannot be compared to any other meal. Jesus hosted this meal in a very special way. He stands for its whole meaning. He began the meal by washing the feet of the disciples. Dirty and sore from long journeys on gravel and stone, the disciples are made clean before reclining at the table with Jesus. It is precisely in this way that even you and I come to the Lord's holy meal, dirty and sore, bruised by everyday journeys through sin, guilt, and shame. But it is just for such men that Jesus has instituted this meal, for sinners who realize their constant need for forgiveness, purification, and nourishment. The words of institution have been heard since the earliest days of the church. Sunday after Sunday, words that clarify who the table is for are repeated: "The Lord Jesus on the night when he was betrayed took bread" (1 Cor. 11:23). It was of course those who reclined at the table with him who would betray and deny him, and yet it was precisely for them that Jesus instituted his meal. Bread and wine were sufficient for this meal, and for all the celebrations of the Lord's Supper from that time forth, as well as for the disciples who would gladly but not always manage to follow their Master. Those who doubt the promise and are ashamed of their confession betray and deny Jesus in their thoughts, words, and deeds. So, he who makes the meal holy is not the guest, but the real presence of the Lord, the host. It is he who invites us to the table, and the gifts he gives are his own body and his own blood, given and shed for you and me for the forgiveness of sins.

For this reason, to eat and drink at the Lord's table in "a worthy manner" (1 Cor. 11:27) does not mean that we are free of sin and worthy in and of ourselves. To go to the Lord's Supper does not mean to claim one's worthiness. Rather by doing this, a Christian confesses that he is a sinner in need of Jesus and the gifts he gives to us by grace alone. If we can admonish a man, who is weighed down with distress and sin to take his refuge and seek help in prayer and the Word, then he is also welcome at the table of grace. The Lord's Supper is a means of grace and as such, it is only for those who need God's grace. Luther's instruction concerning the Lord's Supper makes it clear and obvious. His word is a wonderful comfort for all of us who recognize our unworthiness.

> People with such misgivings must learn that it is the highest art to realize that this sacrament does not depend upon our worthiness. For we are not baptized because we are worthy and holy, nor do we come to confession as if we were pure and without sin; on the contrary, we come as poor miserable people, precisely because we are unworthy. [. . .] But those who earnestly desire grace and comfort should compel themselves to

go and allow no one to deter them, saying, "I would really like to be worthy but I come not on account of any worthiness of mine, but on account of your word." [. . .] This is difficult, however for we always have this obstacle and hindrance to contend with, that we concentrate more upon ourselves than upon the words that come from Christ's lips. [. . .] Here stand the gracious and lovely words, "This is my body, given FOR YOU," "This is my blood shed FOR YOU for the forgiveness of sins." These words, as I have said, are not preached to wood or stone but to you and me [. . .] Ponder, then, and include yourself personally in the "You" so that he may not speak to you in vain. [. . .] But those who feel their weakness, who are anxious to be rid of it and desire help, should regard and use the sacrament as a precious antidote against the poison in their systems. For here in the sacrament you are to receive from Christ's lips the forgiveness of sins, which contains and brings with it God's grace and Spirit with all his gifts, protection, defense, and power against death, the devil, and every trouble. [. . .] go joyfully to the sacrament and let yourself be refreshed, comforted, and strengthened. For if you wait until you are rid of your burden in order to come to the sacrament purely and worthily, you will have to stay away from it forever. In such a case he pronounces the verdict, "If you are pure and upright, you have no need of me and I also have no need of you." Therefore the only ones who are unworthy are those who do not feel their burdens nor admit to being sinners.[5]

The Lord's Supper—An Act of Confession in Faith

The Lord's holy meal gives form to the whole gospel and makes faith physical and concrete. The words of institution—"take eat," "drink of it all of you," and "do this"—signify that this is obviously something we shall *do*. We are not admonished to try and perceive, experience, or feel anything. In the meal, God's good gifts come to us in, with, and under the bread and the wine. The words "as often as you do this" emphasize again that it is a matter of action, and it is understood that this should be repeated often. The fact is that the Lord's Supper is the one part of the divine service that Jesus himself has commanded us to do. Therefore, the Lord's Supper is an inevitable part of both the Christian's life and the life of the church. Here, faith becomes visible and practical. The meal is prepared on the altar, and our focus is directed to physical things and physical actions that form the meaning of the meal. Now the believer may not only hear, but also see, leave their seat and come forward to the altar, perhaps even kneel. She may stretch out her cupped hands, receive, feel, smell, and taste the grace of God in the form of bread and wine. In this way, the gospel is made tangible for all our senses. We often live with a conception that everything that has to do with faith takes the path out from within. We think that that which is authentic must come from our heart and then be expressed in external actions. But with the gospel, it is in fact the opposite. The whole drama of redemption plays out externally to us and our striving. The gospel comes to us from without, and the good news concerning God's grace, free and for nothing, is proclaimed to us completely and wholly without our cooperation. This justification that God gives us is Christ's righteousness and has nothing to do with us, our works, experiences, or feelings. In the same way it is with the

Lord's Supper, which is nothing but the gospel in physical form. Jesus comes to us from without, through bread and wine over which God has spoken his promise. In the Lord's Supper, then, the focus flees from us to God's work through Christ; he comes to us and enters us from without. It is not about evoking feelings in the soul or about more knowledge in the head, but about actions that are repeated and through which the gospel incorporates itself within the body.

The Lord's Supper—A Commemoration

The holy actions of the Lord's Supper remind us of Christ, his life and death, his resurrection, and his ascension. They remind us of his promise and his suffering on the cross for us. In the Lord's Supper, the offense of Golgotha stands before us as a historical fact. When Jesus said, "Do this in memory of me" (Luke 22:19), he anchored the words of institution to the Jewish Passover meal: "This day shall be for you a memorial day, and you shall keep it as a feast to the LORD . . . And you shall observe the Feast of Unleavened Bread, for on this very day I brought your hosts out of the land of Egypt" (Exodus 12:14–17). Just as Israel's people constantly turned back to the blood of the Lamb that freed them from slavery in Egypt, so we remember the Lord's Supper concerning the Lamb of God who takes away the sin of the world on the cross. Paul too connects it to this motif and describes the Lord's Supper from a Jewish perspective. When the house father in the Jewish family addressed the Passover meal and the child asked, "What does this mean and what was it that happened on that night?", then the father of the house tells the story of the blood of the lamb that shielded them from judgment and freed them from Egypt. This is why when Paul repeated the words of institution for the Lord's Supper, he began by answering the question of what happened that night from the perspective of the New Testament: "The Lord Jesus on the night when he was betrayed took bread . . ." (1 Cor. 11:23). That the Lord's Supper is a commemoration does not mean that it should be reduced to a simple remembrance. It is a commemoration where we receive spiritual nourishment. As W. F. Besser so beautifully expresses it:

> The high sacrament of the Lord's Supper is the church's pearl of great price and her most valuable treasure; therein she possesses her only true heirloom. The Lord's Supper is the most comforting testament . . . an inexhaustible spring from which we draw, to learn to know the blessed mystery . . . just as Holy Baptism is the Christian's womb, so the Holy Supper is the mother's breast.[6]

The book by Besser cited above also refers to Luther's words about the Lord's Supper as a commemoration. Luther went right to them, as in his remembrance of Christ's suffering he devoted himself to the accusation of Judas's betrayal. Judas was really "the servant of our sin" when he betrayed Jesus, but it is we who have crucified and killed God's Son through our sins. The Lord's Supper helps us to remember this: it was we who were worthy of death through our trespasses and sins, but it was Christ who took our place under God's wrath and judgment, for our sake.

The Lord's Supper—A Thanksgiving

The Lord's Supper is also called the Eucharist, which means thanksgiving. How can a person do anything but rejoice, thank, and praise God when Christ's sacrifice for us is put before our eyes so clearly and tangibly as it is in the Lord's Supper? The meal is then marked not by any worry or heaviness or self-imposed dignity. That which is really worthy of the celebration of the Lord's Supper is effervescent songs of praise, not gloom. This does not mean raising emotional reactions as a criterion for a true celebration of the Lord's Supper. A person should not evaluate the blessings of the Lord's Supper and retention based on the emotional mood, or the measure of being overcome. In the Lord's Supper, then, we celebrate an objective action that is independent of us and what we subjectively experience as true. Emotionally charged or not, it is still true that we have encountered the Savior in the Lord's Supper and received his greatest gift. So, we come to the Lord's table in thanksgiving and with hymns of praise.

The Lord's Supper—An Act of Communion

At the Lord's table, we fall to our knees before something greater than ourselves. Young and old, women and men, rich and poor, here we are united regardless of class, gender, culture, or ethnicity. We are enveloped and united by this great mystery that contains redemption. The greeting of peace that is part of the communion liturgy is a sign of the redemption that happened through Christ. All that was destroyed by sin is healed in Christ. Through Christ, we are united with God, but also with each other, and not the least with ourselves. Life is still complex and problematic. Conflicts can arise with others, and even within ourselves we feel the effects of sin, but in the Lord's Supper, we are given occasion to lay all conflicts and unsolved problems under the redeeming blood that unites us in Christ. "So we who are many are one body, for we all participate in the same bread." These are words that are spoken when the bread is broken up for the congregation. The bread consists of grain that is blended with water and dissolved and together makes bread. In the same way, the wine consists of many grapes that are pressed into a common drink. Christ's physical body is broken apart in order that Christ's body (the church) should be built up and united. In the Lord's Supper, we confess that we belong to one another, that we are brothers and sisters in the holy communion. This communion reaches past time and space. Here we express our unity with those who have gone before us and are united with all the saints throughout all time. This is a foretaste of the heavenly glory that awaits us.

The Lord's Supper—The True Presence of Jesus

That which makes the greatest difference at the celebration of the Lord's Supper is how a person understands its deepest meaning. If the Lord's Supper is something we do for God rather than something God does for us, if it is a work to perform and not a gift to receive, or if it is simply a symbolic act where Jesus is not present, the meal lacks both its power and its essential meaning. Jesus Christ gives himself to us in the Lord's Supper, his own body and his blood. Concerning this, the church had been in overall agreement up until the sixteenth century. With Zwingli at the lead, the Radical Reformation gave rise to the symbolical interpretation of the Lord's Supper, that is, the view that the Lord's Supper is simply a meal of remembrance where we remember the suffering and death of Jesus for ourselves. Perhaps with this view, it is conceivable that one does not celebrate the Lord's Supper very often. But for those who believe in the real presence of Jesus in the bread and the wine, it is unthinkable to not celebrate the Lord's Supper regularly and often. Luther's words concerning the contents of the Lord's Supper in *The Large Catechism* are clarifying:

> Now, what is the Sacrament of the Altar? Answer: It is the true
> body and blood of the Lord Christ, in and under the bread and

wine, which we Christians are commanded by Christ's word to eat and drink. And just as we said of baptism that it is not mere water, so we say here, too, that the sacrament is bread and wine, but not mere bread and wine such as is served at the table. Rather, it is bread and wine set within God's Word and bound to it.[7]

Reason will always limit the supernatural dimension of faith and empty the meal of the mystery through endless explanations and metaphysical speculations. Can Jesus be present in bread and wine with his body and blood? Either the bread and wine must be changed (transubstantiation) to flesh and blood, or it must then simply mean a "spiritual" presence of Christ. But Lutheran theology holds firm that precisely as through his incarnation Christ is God and man at the same time, so the bread and the wine are at the same time Christ's body and blood. In theological lingo, we speak of two natures that are inseparably united. In the Lord's Supper, that which externally looks as if it is only bread and wine is in reality the host of Christ's body and blood. Where the Lord's Supper is concerned, we lean on the words of institution as Jesus gave them and believe them precisely as they read without attempting to explain them away: "Now as they were eating, Jesus took bread, and after blessing it broke it and gave it to the disciples, and said, 'Take, eat; this is my body." And he took a cup, and when he had given thanks he gave it to them, saying, "Drink of it, all of you, for this is my blood of the covenant, which is poured out for many for the forgiveness of sins'" (Matt. 26:26–28). When John authored his gospel much later, he rendered the words of Jesus in light of the Church's communion: "Whoever feeds on my flesh and drinks my blood has eternal life, and I will raise him up on the last day. For my flesh is true food, and my blood is true drink. Whoever feeds on my flesh and drinks my blood abides in me, and I in him. As the living Father sent me, and I live because of the Father, so whoever feeds on me, he also will live because of me" (John 6:54–57). These were already as challenging at that time as they are today, and they caused many of his disciples to leave him. Yet when he turns to the twelve and asks if even they think this is too much and want to leave, Peter answers: "Lord, to whom shall we go? You have the words of eternal life, and we have believed, and have come to know, that you are the Holy One of God" (John 6:68–69). This is also our faith. Jesus Christ is the Holy One of God, the Lamb of God who takes away the sin of the world. We may go to him, and in the Lord's Supper we encounter him who is the bread of life and hear the words of life: Christ's body broken for you; Christ's blood shed for you. Again, Luther wrote:

> Therefore, it is appropriately called food of the soul, for it nourishes and strengthens the new creature . . . Therefore the Lord's Supper is given as a daily food and sustenance so that our faith may be refreshed and strengthened and that it may not succumb in the struggle but become stronger and stronger. [. . .] Here again our clever spirits contort themselves with their great learning and wisdom; they rant and rave, "How can bread and wine forgive sins or strengthen faith?" Yet they have heard and know that we do not claim this of bread and wine—for in itself bread is bread—but of that bread and wine that are Christ's body and blood and that are accompanied by the Word. These and no other we say are the treasure through which such forgiveness is obtained. This treasure is conveyed and

communicated to us in no other way than through the words, "given and shed for you." [. . .] as if he said, "this is why I give it and bid you eat and drink, that you may take it as your own and enjoy it." All those who let these words be addressed to them and believe that they are true have what the words declare.[8]

The Keys

Concerning the Church's Confession of Sins and the Care of the Soul

Fourth, God's people or holy Christians are recognized by the office of the keys exercised publicly. That is, as Christ decrees in Matthew 18 [.15 20], if a Christian sins, he should be reproved; and if he does not mend his ways he should be bound in his sin and cast out. If he does mend his ways he should be absolved. That is the office of the keys. Now the use of the keys is twofold, public and private. There are some people with consciences so tender and despairing that even if they have not been publicly condemned they cannot find comfort until they have been individually absolved by the pastor . . . Now where you see sins forgiven or reproved in some persons, be it publicly or privately, you may know that God's people are there. If God's people are not there, the keys are not there either; and if the keys are not present for Christ, God's people are not present. Christ bequeathed them as a public sign and a holy possession, whereby the Holy Spirit again sanctifies the fallen sinners redeemed by Christ's death, and whereby the Christians confess that they are a holy people in this world under Christ.[1]

The Reformation—A Soul Care Revival

The proclamation of the Word, baptism in water, and the Lord's Supper are things that all Protestant Christians affirm. With confession, it is quite different; it is rarely associated with the congregational life of evangelicals, at least not in the modern sense of the word evangelical. The early Reformation's leaders laid great emphasis on confession. As Christian Braw has pointed out "The birthplace of the reformation was the confessional chair, not the lectern. For the young Luther, everything revolved around confession."[2] Or as Martin Barth has expressed it: "Luther's theology, whatever else it is, is above all a therapeutic theology [. . .] Luther's writings, therefore, do not belong first of all to the desk, but to the nightstand."[3] Luther's discovery of justification by faith was then not merely the fruit of careful Bible study, but his new understanding of justification also revived his own tortured conscience. So, Luther's work to reform the church was not driven solely by his call as a theologian, but also by his call as a pastor and *seelsorger*.[4] He himself had experienced the freeing power of forgiveness and had compassion for those around him who did not have this certainty concerning the forgiveness of sins. Luther's writings and sermons have an obvious alignment with the care of souls, so that it can be said that the whole of his theology is in service of the guilt-laden conscience. "Comfort" is perhaps the word that Luther most often returned to in his sermons. Luther knew what it meant to be a man in constant struggle with guilt, and here, confession was of great value. Luther never systematized his theology like Thomas Aquinas in *Summa Theologica*, or Philip Melanchthon in *Loci Communes*, or even John Calvin in *Institution Christianae Religionis*. In order to understand Luther's theology, we need to recognize that, more than anyone else, he spoke and wrote from a pastoral perspective as a shepherd for his congregation, concerned with all the ordinary problems that made themselves relevant there. It is precisely this that Carl Axel Aurelius points out in his excellent book *Hjärtpunkten*: "For Luther the point of the keys was not to create clean congregations. That would be Donatism. Instead they should be used in pastoral care. They are given for this purpose. [. . .] to not use the keys is poor soul care."[5]

In the *Augsburg Confession*, confession is mentioned in direct connection with the sacraments, baptism, and the Lord's Supper. The placement of confession in this doctrinal document says something about the central place the reformers gave to confession in the life of the church. As we read in the Confession: "Concerning confession they teach that the private absolution should be retained in the churches."[6] Confession is then no end in itself. Precisely as is true concerning the Word, baptism, the Lord's Supper and even the office (the subject of the next chapter), confession is given as a comfort and assurance of the forgiveness of sins. When confession falls into oblivion and is not used, something essential is lacking in our daily fight against sin. But when the preaching of law and gospel is heard loud and clear and God's Spirit awakens man, confession becomes essential. When a person becomes conscious of sin and the serious questions concerning guilt and forgiveness start to test your soul, it is important that the servants of the church hold up the significance of confession and give opportunity for it. But first, it must be grounded in pastors who themselves have experienced the blessings of personal confession and absolution. He who does not regularly go to confession can hardly instruct or invite the members of the church to confession.

The Daily Fight Against Sin

> Blessed is the one whose transgression is forgiven,
> whose sin is covered.
> Blessed is the man against whom the LORD counts no iniquity,
> and in whose spirit there is no deceit.
> For when I kept silent, my bones wasted away
> through my groaning all day long.
> For day and night your hand was heavy upon me;
> my strength was dried up as by the heat of summer. Selah
> I acknowledged my sin to you,
> and I did not cover my iniquity;
> I said, "I will confess my transgressions to the LORD,"
> and you forgave the iniquity of my sin. Selah (Psalm 32:1–5)

These words of the Psalmist, which are over 3,000 years old, set their finger on a problem that also weighs on the modern man. But the words not only describe the problem, they also describe the solution. Beatitude, freedom, and joy characterize the person who experiences the freeing power of forgiveness, the wonderful certainty that this sin is atoned for and forgiven. All honest Christians recognize themselves in the Psalmist's words concerning the burden of sin and the gnawing conscience. When this does not receive a resolution, we have no peace and no freedom, we lose desire and concentration at work. Our thoughts are consumed until we fall asleep in the evening, and first thing in the morning, they are terrorized again by torturous thoughts, angst concerning that which ought not to have been said or done. The unresolved conflicts hang in the air, the embarrassing secrets and lies that we fear will come to light every day. The guilty conscience is occupied with all sorts of things: cheating, betrayal, and unforgiveness that become unresolved trauma burdening the heart. This condition keeps people away from engaging in worship and prayer, not to mention Bible study. It hampers social relations, dams up our joy, inhibits boldness, and casts a dark shadow over the whole of one's existence. In the deepest sense, all this is the result of our guilt before God, which is itself the root of the problem.

The Psalmist gives voice to this dark experience: "For when I kept silent . . ." So, it is the silence, that we hide and suppress our guilt, that keeps us in this miserable condition. "Day and night your hand was heavy upon me, my strength dried up . . ." What can then turn this lament into joy again? What can free the soul from this dark prison and let the light in? For far too many people, the solution is to remain silent. We fear what others would say if they knew how it really was with us. Some keep silent only because they do not have anyone to speak with under safe and ordered forms. They simply do not know where they should turn with their pain. Silence and suppression become extra burdens that are laid upon the already heavy weight of guilt. The wonderful words of the Psalter speak directly to this: "I acknowledged my sin to you, and I did not cover my iniquity. I said, 'I will confess my transgressions to the Lord.' And you forgave the iniquity of my sin." Most people have at one time or another experienced the freedom of confession and coming out of hiding. Lies and excuses might fool those around us, even those closest to us, but never one's own conscience. In response to the grace of the gospel, we can confess our sins before God privately. But confession is more concrete because it is done before another listening soul. In confession, there is a dimension to our experience that is often more real and definitive. The Church has therefore done tortured people a disservice by being quiet about confession and withholding opportunity to relieve all the burdens that they carry. Therefore, this mark of the church needs to be reestablished so that miserable and plagued souls can be freed and experience God's forgiveness and grace.

The Keys in Soul Care

> And behold, some people brought to him a paralytic, lying on a bed. And when Jesus saw their faith, he said to the paralytic, "Take heart, my son; your sins are forgiven." And behold, some of the scribes said to themselves, "This man is blaspheming." But Jesus, knowing their thoughts, said, "Why do you think evil in your hearts? For which is easier, to say, 'Your sins are forgiven,' or to say, 'Rise and walk'? But that you may know that the Son of Man has authority on earth to forgive sins"—he then said to the paralytic— "Rise, pick up your bed and go home." And he rose and went home. When the crowds saw it, they were afraid, and they glorified God, who had given such authority to men (Matt. 9:2–8).

When Luther expounds upon this gospel text, he writes that we are all like the lame man in the narrative. The paralysis is our pain under the oppressive force of sin and guilt. Just as the lame man's limbs are atrophied and unusable so that he cannot freely move, man's soul is fettered and weighed down by sin before God. But the gospel's joyous news is that there is one who has power to free us from our sin. He who suffers under the pangs of conscience and struggles with his angst may come to Jesus, where he can receive wonderful help. What can be more glorious for an anxious soul than to hear, loud and clear, the words of Jesus, "Take heart, my son; your sins are forgiven"? But where and through whom may we then hear these wonderful words of grace and forgiveness today? Let us hear what Luther had to say about this:

As we heard, this power has come to the world through Jesus Christ. And it has remained with us men. This applies especially for those in the office and who have this commission, that they shall proclaim the gospel, that is repentance and the forgiveness of sins in the name of Jesus. [. . .] You have the right to comfort yourself with such words, just as if Christ himself had spoken them to you from heaven. [. . .] Learn then to speak about the forgiveness of sins and instruct others about it in this way: "In baptism, in absolution, in the pulpit and in the Lord's Supper God speaks to us through the church's servants or through some other Christian. This is what we should believe when we receive the forgiveness of sins. For here it is written, that the forgiveness of sins is a power that is given to men here on earth, where one baptizes, distributes the Lord's Supper, absolves and preaches from the pulpit." This is to truly help people come to God and to the forgiveness of sins.[7]

During the earthly life of Jesus, he walked about preaching, healing the sick, and giving the forgiveness of sins. A repetitious word from the lips of Jesus in the encounter of mangled men is the absolution: "Your sins are forgiven!" After the resurrection of Jesus, he gave his disciples the same power to distribute the forgiveness of sins: "Jesus said to them again, 'Peace be with you. As the Father has sent me, even so I am sending you.' And when he had said this, he breathed on them and said to them, 'Receive the Holy Spirit. If you forgive the sins of any, they are forgiven them; if you withhold forgiveness from any, it is withheld'" (John 20:21–23). Just as both baptism and the Lord's Supper are instituted by Christ, here we have what we could call the words of institution for confession and absolution. In Lutheran theology, this is called the *power of the keys.* Jesus himself has given his church the keys to the kingdom of heaven, and they shall be used by his called and consecrated servants. They are called the keys because this is the word Jesus himself used concerning this commission: "I will build my church, and the gates of hell shall not prevail against it. I will give you the keys of the kingdom of heaven, and whatever you bind on earth shall be bound in heaven, and whatever you loose on earth shall be loosed in heaven" (Matt. 16:18–19). When the keys are used, people are freed from sin, guilt, and shame. The translation of the Greek word for forgiveness (*afesis*) has a relatively weak meaning. The Greek word has a richer meaning than to simply remit sins and includes to strike out, take away from, free, set free, and take from you. Luther's words on the power of the keys are clarifying:

> Here we have the command that one should maintain the preaching of Jesus Christ, that sins should be forgiven for all those who believe in him. [. . .] This is a great and marvelous thing, that every righteous shepherd and preacher's mouth is the mouth of Christ, and his words and forgiveness, the words and forgiveness of Christ. If you have sins, but confess them and believe in Christ, then in the stead of Christ the preacher shall forgive these sins, and this word which he says to you on behalf of God shall be received by you as if Christ himself had spoken them to you. So one is right to call the word that

preacher preaches God's Word. For it is not the preacher's office and word, but God's own.[8]

Thus, the keys are a tool for evangelical church-life and a mark of the Christian church, a liberating power instituted by Jesus himself. It is also fitting to call this means the keys. With keys, a man opens something that was shut. People can feel bound and locked in their sin. They find themselves imprisoned by their guilt-laden conscience. Yet, just as they are sitting there, locked and isolated in their sins, the words of forgiveness are spoken and they are freed by the power of the keys that the church possesses to unfetter, unlock, and open.

Confession—Private Confession and Personal Absolution

Why is it not sufficient with the confession of sins and the absolution that is offered publicly in our corporate worship? Why do we need to provide private confession? Lutheran theologians have sometimes used the following picture to illustrate the difference between forgiveness in the divine service and in private confession. Preaching is compared with a man who throws a handful of gold coins into a group of people. Some may grab them, others do not, or they hesitate and stay outside. But in private confession, it is different. There, it is as if an emissary comes to a particular individual person, presses a gold coin in his hand, and says: "I received a commission from my Lord to give this precisely to you. Take and hold on to it!" Private confession therefore makes it easier for a depressed and burdened human being to receive the forgiveness of sins and thereby receive a certainty concerning the forgiveness of sins so that he can actually stop fretting. In private confession, God punches holes in the false and dangerous thought, supported by the accusations and lies of Satan, that the promise of Jesus concerning the forgiveness of sins does not apply to me and my grave transgressions. Oh, what a comfort and benefit to be assured of the forgiveness of sins in confession and to be able to quit wavering back and forth. We can also worry ourselves over things that actually do not need the forgiveness of sins. In those situations, it is helpful to have an experienced pastor or *Seelsorger*. Someone who can listen to our thoughts in order to help us sort out between actual sins and things that are merely monsters of the imagination or weaknesses. In that way, we can be delivered from false guilt and rest assured that we can leave behind those kinds of thoughts without worry.

Confession—A Sacrament of Joy

In many Christian traditions, confession is called a sacrament. As we saw above, confession is mentioned in connection with baptism and the Lord's Supper in *The Augsburg Confession*. The reformers described confession as sacramental because it mediates God's grace and forgiveness on the basis of God's promise concerning the forgiveness of sins. A person often reserves the designation of sacrament for baptism and the Lord's Supper, but confession can also be called sacrament at times because it is an extension of the sacrament of baptism. In *The Large Catechism*, Luther said that baptism "comprehends the third sacrament, formerly called penance, which is really nothing else than baptism."[9] It is not infrequent that confession is also called *the sacrament of joy*. There may be some discomfort associated with going to confession. But the joy that follows the personal and concrete forgiveness of sins is a freeing experience which far transcends the initial discomfort.

Perhaps we can compare confession with something as common as cleaning. There is an aversion to start cleaning when we see all the dirt and mess. One does not know where to begin when junk fills the entire room. But what a glorious joy there is hidden in the simple, but sometimes mundane act of clearing out a space. People often look very happy at a heap of garbage on a Saturday morning. They have finally made a dent in the matter and determined to clean up and throw out everything that is cluttering the house, clearing out storage rooms and garages of things that constrain their original use. In the same way, there is an insight from psychology concerning the health benefits for both body and soul to clean out one's worries and disappointments in order to ease the conscience. In confession, though, something happens that far transcends what psychology can do for us. The strongholds of angst and worry are pulled up by the roots. Instead of fleeing from the problem or inventing excuses, we can own up and pull them into the light and there find forgiveness, joy, and freedom.

Confession—Gospel, Not Law

During the Reformation, confession was not done away with, but rather the reformers began to instruct about it in the clear light of the gospel. They described confession as a place where a person encounters the promise of the gospel concerning the forgiveness of sins and receives God's grace. It can be seen that confession was very precious to Luther himself when he said: "I will let no one take away private confession and would not exchange it for all the wealth of the world, for I know what strength and comfort it has given me."[10] On the other hand, the Reformation abolished the compulsion to go to confession and the requirement to confess all sins. The reformers quite simply understood that it was not possible for a man to remember all the sins he had committed in thought, word, and deed. Instead, confession was presented as a wonderful invitation, not as a demand. Like all God's ordinances, confession is there to help us and bless us. It shall not be understood as a pious work that we must do for God, even if God looks with great delight on the confession of our sins. Paul Althaus summarizes Luther's position on confession: "Luther rejects the ecclesiastical rule which requires confession. It cannot be made a law, but it is an indispensable form of the gospel. It is therefore not a requirement but rather a gift which we cannot do without." Confession also presupposes a pastor is present, and this is something that Luther strongly emphasized. He was critical of pastors for neither living nor dwelling among the people, and repulsed that many of the Lord's servants had taken refuge in the cloisters. Confession was to be possible every day, and this required pastors to be present and involved in daily congregational life. To make use of Luther's description of Christ's presence in the bread and the wine of the Lord's Supper, one can say that Luther believed in the pastor's real presence in and among his congregation.

Confession—A Means of Health

Confession does not consist of long deep conversations, nor of loud cries and intense prayers. It consists of two simple parts: confession and absolution. In his confession of sins, an individual gets to hear and receive forgiveness from God himself through the audible voice of another and be assured that he need not doubt it. In the evangelical confession of sins, there is no emphasis that a person should dig and grovel in their sins. A person should confess that which lies on their heart, those sins a person is conscious of at that moment, those that are stressing them out or torturing them. The pastor leads confession with the help of a simple order, and the experienced caretaker of souls knows exactly what it is all about. Before sin and grace, we are all the same, and he who knows the darkness of his own heart is not dismayed by another man's sin. He who speaks the gospel's promise of the forgiveness of sins does not represent himself, but he is the instrument of Christ and commissioned by the church. The pastor uses the keys which Christ himself has given him, and it is the ears of Christ that hear confessions and Christ's mouth that speaks the forgiveness of sins through him.

Neither does confessing mean to dwell in one's sin but to regret it. A man carries a desire to be free from the guilt that gnaws at him, and he wants to have God's grace and forgiveness. Sin inhibits us and destroys our relationship to God, man, and even ourselves. Shame grows and builds a wall, isolating us from the world around us, causing us to be turned in on ourselves. Confession helps liberate us and reestablish us as human beings. The more specific our confession is, the more obvious is the forgiveness for us. A crucial insight at confession is that one stands before Jesus Christ. Therefore, confession is characterized by both grace and truth. Truth without grace is brutal; grace without truth is only sentimental and ineffectual. Confession is also often the start of a healing process that takes time. We should not expect an instant miracle through which we are finally finished with our fight against sin. That freedom waits until the day of resurrection. A person who continues to carry unresolved sin and guilt that is not managed encounters the future with fear. He who is forgiven can meet the future with confidence. Confession assures us of God's grace and forgiveness, establishes us in the peace of God, and helps us in our Christian walk.

Questions about Confession

Is it really evangelical to go to confession?

It is very evangelical to go to confession because confession builds upon and deals with the actual kernel of the gospel: the forgiveness of sins. You confess that you are a sinner and that Christ is your savior. In and of yourself, you can do nothing but remain in sin, but through God's grace, you are forgiven and accounted righteous for the sake of Jesus Christ through faith. This is nothing other than the gospel in a very personal and concrete form.

To whom shall one confess?

Naturally, an individual can open his heart to whichever brother or sister he trusts. But there is no security in a vow of silence, or certainty that the one who listens has experience or is equipped to give me that which I really need: certainty concerning the forgiveness of my sins. So, it is normal to go to a congregational pastor for confession. In the church, there ought to be suitable spaces where this can be done undisturbed and with a good order under the supervision of a consecrated and experienced *Seelsorger*.

When can one go to confession?

There is no particular time or rule for confession. But the short answer is: when it is needed. During the seasons of fasting at Advent and Lent, it is natural to go to confession because it is a time of repentance for the whole church. Other occasions that are natural for confession are in the case of severe falls, or when we go through tests and doubts and crises of different sorts. But also, in periods of spiritual awakening, there may be need for confession.

How should one confess?

Book a time with your pastor. Prepare yourself during the time before confession. Aim to be very brief and specific at confession. Confess your particular sins without excuses or pointing to aggravating circumstances. Then receive and trust in the absolution and use this blessing as a weapon in the fight against all Satan's lies and accusations.

But does not living as a Christian mean that one has quit sinning?

One of the great insights of the Reformation was that which Luther formulated in the words *simul iustus et peccator*, that is, that the Christian is always simultaneously righteous and sinner. This is not an excuse to take sin lightly. Sin is serious, and he who plays with it will experience its deadly poison. The Apostle John answers this question indirectly when in his first letter he wrote:

> But if we walk in the light, as he is in the light, we have fellow-ship with one another, and the blood of Jesus his Son cleanses us from all sin. If we say we have no sin, we deceive ourselves, and the truth is not in us. If we confess our sins, he is faithful and just to forgive us our sins and to cleanse us from all unrighteousness . . . My little children, I am writing these things to you so that you may not sin. But if anyone does sin, we have an advocate with the Father, Jesus Christ the righteous. He is the propitiation for our sins, and not for ours only but also for the sins of the whole world (1 John 1:7–9; 2:1–2).

I will let my good friend, pastor Håkan Sunnliden from whose book *The Church—God's Gift* I have gathered great inspiration for this chapter, finish this section on the power of the keys. Sunnliden answers the question: "Ought not the Christian finally walk in victory?" He answers: "Yes, but a Christian who lives in true knowledge of himself and dares to live in the confession of sins and faith in God's Word, he walks in victory. Not he who is constantly forced to repress and deny reality, and makes use of pious masks with which he constantly justifies himself."[11]

The Office

Concerning the Church's Called and Ordained Servants

Fifth, the church is recognized externally by the fact that it consecrates or calls ministers, or has offices that it is to administer. There must be bishops, pastors, or preachers, who publicly and privately give, administer, and use the aforementioned four things or holy possessions in behalf of and in the name of the church, or rather by reason of their institution by Christ, as St. Paul states in Eph. 4 [:8], "He received gifts among men . . ."— his gifts were that some should be apostles, some prophets, some evangelists, some teachers and governors, etc. The people as a whole cannot do these things, but must entrust or have them entrusted to one person. Otherwise, what would happen if everyone wanted to speak or administer, and no one wanted to give way to the other? It must be entrusted to one person, and he alone should be allowed to preach, to baptize, to absolve, and to administer the sacraments.[1]

A Lost Concept

Today the concept of the *office* is felt to be a bit archaic and is seldom used in everyday conversation. But for the church, it is held to be something important that needs to be recovered. The actual word "office" is not a biblical term, even if it appears in a few places in the Swedish Bible translation. The more biblical terms are "ministry" or "commission." But here, it is not the term we are after, but the actual concept. This concept is in Scripture from the very beginning, and it exists even today in a certain variation in the design and designation of the leading commission in the Christian congregations. In the landscape of the early Christian church, a person can discern a rather unified model with bishops, priests (pastors), and deacons. Already in the pastoral epistles, we see that this order is beginning to develop. In international ecumenism, these ministries are commonly called *clergy*, the church's *ordained ministry*. This is why I use the concept "office" here as a term for the people who are ordained or consecrated in the church for a special commission.

In our day-to-day language, the concept of the office is linked to thoughts of representation and authorization, as when one represents a public authority of some sort. In other words, a man cannot take on an office himself. He is ordained to it and can thereby speak and operate "in the authority of his office." In order to understand the role of the office, we might think about certain professions in the secular life that have representatives and authoritative functions. For example, a legal representative or an advocate represents and carries someone else's case in a legal dispute. The advocate's authority does not rest on his or her personality or talent, but on a formal training and an official authorization in the form of an office, an advocate's license bestowed by a legal society or bar. The advocate is obligated to follow good juridical customs, and the bar has responsibility for ongoing review and oversight, even taking disciplinary measures and even withdrawing the license if the office is abused. The police officer also has an obvious authoritative and representative function that is regulated by law and stands under the authorities of the government. It is not just anyone who can act as a police officer when someone goes over the speed limit; it is only the authorized police who have this authority. The role of the office in the case of a police officer is also linked to a certain way of dress, a police uniform. When we listen to the police officer's decree, it is not the private person behind the uniform we obey, but the office that the uniform signals and represents. Behind the uniform, the police officer is like any other person, and without the uniform, we do not perceive the office. Through education, training, and testing, he has received his legitimization and is given the right within the confines of the law to act as a police officer with high authority.

We would be able to continue this with other examples or roles that have the character of an office, for example, a soccer referee, a judge, or city councils that all have a representative and authoritative function within a limited area. I find myself writing in the USA. There is currently a heated discussion here concerning the present occupant of the land's highest office, the presidential office. Regardless of which view a person has concerning the person behind the presidency, it is fascinating to see what great respect everyone has for the actual office. The office's authority really does not lie in the person but in the American Constitution. It is just because this office is so important that the critiques are so hard when the person behind the office seems unfit.

An Office from God

With these introductory words concerning the concept of the office with examples from secular life, we shall now devote ourselves to the office from an ecclesiastical perspective and as a mark of the Christian church. As it says in the Augsburg Confession: "So that we may obtain this faith, the ministry of teaching the gospel and administering the sacraments was instituted."[2] So this office has been instituted in order to mediate that which the earlier chapters dealt with: the Word, Baptism, the Lord's Supper and Confession. There must be an order that ensures that the gospel is proclaimed purely and the sacraments are administered properly; therefore, it is not up to individual pastors to find suitable arrangements for themselves and form their own orders. We encounter this concept of the office in both the Old and the New Testaments. To hold an office in the biblical sense rests upon an order that is instituted by God, where God calls and equips persons for specific tasks. But it is not sufficient that one feels called by God; the call must be recognized within the sphere where one shall serve. In the old Israel, this was as king, prophet, or priest, and in the church, as apostle, prophet, evangelist, pastor, or teacher, thus the office of preaching. In the old Israel, God constituted and consecrated different offices, for example, priests and Levites, to represent him and serve his people. They were given offices to administer his commands and the sacrifices—law and gospel—which were instituted for the salvation and sanctification of the people.

It is very early in the biblical accounts of history that we come across the office of the priesthood in the story of Abraham: "Melchizedek king of Salem brought out bread and wine. (He was priest of God Most High.) And he blessed him" (Gen. 4:18–19). So, Melchizedek was an authorized representative of God who spoke, blessed, and shared gifts on God's behalf. Here, already, the pastoral office is associated with the sharing of bread and wine. The author of Hebrews returned to Melchizedek and used him as a picture of Christ and his high-priestly service in heaven, and here, we are given many insights concerning what the office meant in the Old Testament. Above all, the author of Hebrews described Christ as our high priest in that he has offered himself as a sacrifice for us, in contrast to the priests in the cult of sacrifice who offered the blood of animals in order to atone for the sins of the people. But the primary task of all priests, both before and after Christ, is to represent Christ and point forward (OT) or backward (NT) to Christ as the Lamb of God who takes away the sins of the world. It was through the sacrifices that priests of the Old Testament performed, proclaimed, and mediated a salvation that lay ahead of them. Through the bread and the wine in the Lord's Supper, pastors of the New Testament proclaim and mediate the redemption that was once and for all fulfilled through the atoning work of Christ on the cross, for us.

> For every high priest chosen from among men is appointed to act on behalf of men in relation to God, to offer gifts and sacrifices for sins . . . And no one takes this honor for himself, but only when called by God, just as Aaron was. So also Christ did not exalt himself to be made a high priest, but was appointed by him who said to him, "You are my Son, today I have begotten you"; as he says also in another place, "You are a priest forever, after the order of Melchizedek" (Heb. 5:1, 4–6).

Throughout the historical accounts of the Bible, various forms for the future practice, commissioning, and consecrating of people to the different offices of the church are noticeable. But the order that comes to the forefront is that the call comes from God, and that it is then recognized within the sphere where the office shall be carried out. No one can take an office upon himself according to his own power and will. It is God who chooses, calls, and equips. In the New Testament, it is the church and, finally, Christ who confirms and deposits his office. Jesus chose and called twelve of his disciples to be his apostles. All apostles were disciples, but not all disciples were apostles (Luke 6:12–13). The apostles, in turn, appointed persons for the office after Christ's resurrection and ascension, who with a common concept would be called to be leaders of the congregations. Different words are used for these leaders, but they all point to a similar function: *presbyteros* (which in English is translated as "elder"; it is also the root of the Swedish word for "priest") and *episcopos* (which is translated as the word "overseer" and from which we get the word "bishop" in English). This office and chain of authorized servants continues through the Church's history, first via Timothy and Titus and then on throughout history to our own day. This is an unbroken chain of the office that has been carried on in the church from generation to generation through the laying on of hands and ordination to ministry. It is called *apostolic succession.* The succession ties together the whole of Christ's church through the centuries and the continents into one single great sum. However, the succession does not only deal with the office; ultimately, it deals with that which the office should mediate, namely, the gospel. Even more important than the succession of the office, then, is that which is called the doctrinal succession. Bo Giertz, who himself placed great value on the apostolic succession, warns that it can be carried too far: "We should be careful not to exaggerate the importance of episcopal succession. We cannot ascribe to it any decisive significance for a valid celebration of the Lord's Supper."[3]

We are in this chain of the Lord's servants throughout history, not because we are completely sure concerning exactly who laid their hands upon whom, but because we administer the apostolic commission and proclaim the apostolic message—the gospel—in Word, water, bread, and wine. As it is expressed in the *Apology of the Augsburg Confession*:

> The opponents do not consider the priesthood as a ministry of the word and of the sacraments administered to others. Instead, they consider it as a sacrificial office, as if there ought to be in the New Testament a priesthood similar to the Levitical priesthood, which offers sacrifices for the people and merits the forgiveness of sins for other people. We teach that the sacrificial death of Christ on the cross was sufficient for the sins of the entire world and that there is no need for additional sacrifices, as though Christ's sacrifice was not sufficient for our sins. Therefore, human beings are justified not on account of any other sacrifice except the one sacrifice of Christ when they believe that they have been redeemed by that sacrifice. Thus priests are not called to offer sacrifices for the people as in Old Testament law so that through them they might merit the forgiveness of sins for the people; instead they are called to preach the gospel and to administer the sacraments to the people.[4]

The Common Priesthood of All Believers

Before we explain any further the meaning of the office that serves the church by proclaiming the gospel and administrating the sacraments, we will turn our attention to the ministry that every Christian has. To reserve the word "priest" for simply those who serve the congregation with Word and sacrament is kind of missing the mark. In the New Testament, all Christians are called priests. All of God's people are called to portray and convey the gospel of Jesus Christ. As it says in First Peter:

> You yourselves like living stones are being built up as a spiritual house, to be a holy priesthood, to offer spiritual sacrifices acceptable to God through Jesus Christ . . . But you are a chosen race, a royal priesthood, a holy nation, a people for his own possession, that you may proclaim the excellencies of him who called you out of darkness into his marvelous light. Once you were not a people, but now you are God's people; once you had not received mercy, but now you have received mercy" (1 Pet. 2:5, 9–10).

Thus, through baptism, all believers are placed as "priests" who offer "spiritual sacrifices" and "proclaim his excellencies." This concept was recovered during the Reformation, which emphasized that it was not only priests, monks, and nuns who bore spiritual value or tasks. Every believer in the New Testament is called to present their "bodies as a living sacrifice, holy and acceptable to God, which is your spiritual worship" (Romans 12:1). With these words, Paul referenced the Old Testament priestly ministry that offered sacrifices which atoned for sin and pleased God. But in the New Testament, we are atoned for by Christ's sacrifice and present ourselves, the whole of our lives and all that means, as a "living sacrifice," and there, we may "proclaim God's excellencies." In this manner, all believers are priests, upon whom God bestows various gifts and an important commission. In other words, a person can say that every believer in the New Testament lives his whole life by God's grace to God's glory. However, this does not mean that all believers should be preachers or administrate the sacraments and lead the congregations. God has instituted various orders in his church so that these commissions should be administered and actualized as God wants. As we read in Ephesians:

> But grace was given to each one of us according to the measure of Christ's gift . . . And he gave the apostles, the prophets, the evangelists, the shepherds and teachers, to equip the saints for the work of ministry, for building up the body of Christ, until we all attain to the unity of the faith and of the knowledge of the Son of God, to mature manhood, to the measure of the stature of the fullness of Christ . . . from whom the whole body, joined and held together by every joint with which it is equipped, when each part is working properly, makes the body grow so that it builds itself up in love (Eph. 4:7, 11–13, 16).

To Represent Christ

So, Christ himself gives the office as a gift to some who are to "build up the body of Christ." This means the office is not something that an individual possesses or owns. The office belongs to Christ and, accordingly, to his body, the church. It is not a career that anyone chooses, but a call that one receives from Christ and which is confirmed by the church. The pastor does not represent himself or his own views but is a representative of Christ. He does not speak in the power of his own inspiration or experiences. The words he mediates are Christ's words in the power of the Spirit, and the only work he boasts of is the work of Christ. As Jesus said to his disciples: "The one who hears you hears me, and the one who rejects you rejects me, and the one who rejects me rejects him who sent me" (Luke 10:16). Paul was on the same trail when he spoke about his office in the following way:

> Therefore, having this ministry by the mercy of God, we do not lose heart. But we have renounced disgraceful, underhanded ways. We refuse to practice cunning or to tamper with God's word, but by the open statement of the truth we would commend ourselves to everyone's conscience in the sight of God . . . For what we proclaim is not ourselves, but Jesus Christ as Lord, with ourselves as your servants for Jesus' sake (2 Cor. 4:1–2, 5).

Paul continued to develop the meaning of the office, saying: "Therefore, we are ambassadors for Christ, God making his appeal through us. We implore you on behalf of Christ, be reconciled to God" (2 Cor. 5:20). This office carries with it a great responsibility and is not something to be taken lightly. In our day, as in all ages, there is reason to test oneself against the background of the words of Scripture. To have a God-given office cannot be regarded as one job among others. It is a holy calling from God that one administers, and the "employer" to whom he will one day give account is God himself (Heb. 13:17).

Stewardship

Stewardship is a central theme of the Bible. Of all that we have, including our very own lives, there is nothing we own; we are but stewards of it all. In the highest degree, the office is about stewardship. A steward does not present himself as a lord but proceeds as a servant. That which he administers is something that is entrusted to him, but it belongs to the Lord in whose service he stands and according to whose directive he serves. There is no place here for taking liberties or personal benefits. Jesus himself said: "Who then is the faithful and wise manager, whom his master will set over his household, to give them their portion of food at the proper time? Blessed is that servant whom his master will find so doing when he comes. Truly, I say to you, he will set him over all his possessions'" (Luke 12:42–44). Foundationally, the office deals with devoting oneself to the "ministry of word and prayer" (Acts 6:4). At the center of this task stands prayer and preaching, administration of the sacraments, the care of souls, the reception of confession, and delivery of absolution; this is spiritual leadership. To point to Christ in all things and "equip the saints for the work of ministry, for building up the body of Christ, until we all attain to the unity of the faith and of the knowledge of the Son of God, to mature manhood, to the measure of the stature of the fullness of Christ" (Eph. 4:11–13).

The office administrates God's good gifts for the benefit of the congregation and may not be used for one's own personal benefit. Thus, it is completely wrong to say that the pastor "has a congregation." It is rather the congregation that has a pastor. The church is God's congregation, and he places servants in it whom he has called to administer the gospel and faithfully serve the flock in accordance with God's designated ordinances. When we speak in terms of "the flock," we encounter the biblical concept of a shepherd. The office is often compared with the shepherd's role, and in both Scripture and the history of the church, a pastor is called a "shepherd of the congregation." Here we can think of Psalm 23 where David, who himself was a shepherd, saw the Lord as the good shepherd through the eyes of the sheep. Under the shepherd's care, he is secure and lacks nothing, regardless of whether the path leads to green meadows or through the valley of the shadow of death. The Lord prepares a table and invites one to a meal that gives strength and refreshment. In John 10:11, Jesus said, "I am the good shepherd. The good shepherd lays down his life for the sheep," identifying himself as the Lord in Psalm 23. In the following sections, let's take a closer look at what the office of the shepherd means.

The Office of the Shepherd

When, towards the end of his life, Paul found himself in Ephesus, he gathered those who had a specific responsibility to serve and lead the congregation (Acts 20:17). He began his speech by describing the content of this ministry as God's servant and by reminding them of his own example.

> And when they came to him, he said to them: "You yourselves know how I lived among you the whole time from the first day that I set foot in Asia, serving the Lord with all humility and with tears and with trials that happened to me through the plots of the Jews; how I did not shrink from declaring to you anything that was profitable, and teaching you in public and from house to house, testifying both to Jews and to Greeks of repentance toward God and of faith in our Lord Jesus Christ" (Acts 20:18–21).

Paul also said that his life has no value in and of itself, that he was not driven by any selfish motive, but that he only wished to fulfill the task that the Lord Jesus had given him to administer: "To testify to the gospel of the grace of God" (Acts 20:24). Paul performed his ministry under constant death threats, but for him "to live is Christ, and to die is gain" (Phil. 1:21). So, he could also say to these congregational leaders, both as a summary of his own ministry and as a serious admonition: "I did not shrink from declaring to you the whole counsel of God" (Acts 20:27). Thus, Paul had not been occupied by what made him popular or what produced quick and fancy results. Here, we hear the echo from the serious admonition he gave to Timothy, who for a time served this very same congregation in Ephesus:

> [P]reach the word; be ready in season and out of season; reprove, rebuke, and exhort, with complete patience and teaching. For the time is coming when people will not endure sound teaching, but having itching ears they will accumulate for themselves teachers to suit their own passions, and will turn away from listening to the truth and wander off into myths. As for you, always be sober-minded, endure suffering, do the work of an evangelist, fulfill your ministry (2 Tim. 2:4–5).

We ought to give heed to these words even in our own days. The offices may not be reduced so that the pastor becomes some sort of comforting uncle, social worker, lecturer, or a general project leader. The church is in the midst of a spiritual war, and the threat comes from both within and from without. Paul continued: "I know that after my departure fierce wolves will come in among you, not sparing the flock; and from among your own selves will arise men speaking twisted things, to draw away the disciples after them" (Acts 20:29–30). One of the shepherd's foundational tasks is to protect sheep from wolves and to be able to distinguish them even from those that come dressed up "like sheep." He gave the admonition: "Pay careful attention to yourselves and to all the flock, in which the Holy Spirit has made you overseers, to care for the church of God, which he obtained with his own blood" (Acts 20:28).

My point with these serious words is not to create a gloomy picture of the office, but I believe that it is important that we understand the holy seriousness that surrounds the office, and which is unfortunately all too seldom emphasized in our day. This seriousness rests upon the following things. First, the church belongs to God, not us, and it has cost him the blood of his only begotten and beloved Son to acquire it. Second, he calls this congregation a flock. A flock must be led, protected, and cared for. Without a shepherd, the sheep get lost, get stuck in the bushes, find neither pasture nor water, and do not have much to defend themselves with when the wolves come. Third, it is God himself who, through the Holy Spirit, has instituted the office and called persons to lead this flock as shepherds. This is seldom a glamorous job. It is not something someone seeks if he does not feel himself forced by the call of the Holy Spirit. Paul briefly highlighted some aspects of what this means: "Therefore be alert, remembering that for three years I did not cease night or day to admonish every one with tears" (Acts 20:31). In the same way, Peter described the office. When in the autumn of his life, he admonished the elders (*presbyteroi*) to "shepherd the flock of God that is among you, exercising oversight, not under compulsion, but willingly, as God would have you; not for shameful gain, but eagerly; not domineering over those in your charge, but being examples to the flock" (1 Pet. 5:2–3).

Consecrated by Prayer and the Laying on of Hands

But if ordination is understood with reference to the ministry of the Word, we have no objection to calling ordination a sacrament. For the ministry of the Word has the command of God and has magnificent promises like Romans 1[:16]: "the gospel is the power of God for salvation to everyone who has faith." Likewise, Isaiah 55[:11], ". . . so shall my word be that goes out from my mouth; it shall not return to me empty, but it shall accomplish that which I purpose . . ." If ordination is understood in this way, we will not object to calling the laying on of hands a sacrament. For the church has the mandate to appoint ministers, which ought to please us greatly because we know that God approves this ministry and is present in it.[5]

Ordination is observed as a sacrament in many ecclesiastical traditions. And, I would argue, there really is a sacramental dimension to this holy and serious event. All ecclesiastical traditions use some form of distinction that makes the ministry, which a congregational leader or preacher must perform, visible and possible. In the *Augsburg Confession*, it expressly says: "Concerning church government it is taught that no one should publicly teach, preach or administer the sacraments without a proper [public] call."[6] It is next to impossible to work in the office without a public and visible distinction. Clothing associated with the office is part of this visibility. People need to be able to see who the pastor is; they should not be left to guess. Because the office is a public ministry, the distinction ought also to be public and formally celebrated with a distinguished ceremony. So also, a good liturgy common to the Christian church renders the distinction and clearly embodies the meaning. A visible distinction for service also gives boldness to those who carry it out, and it creates security in the congregation. The bishop, or in other cases the leader of the ecclesiastical body of churches, should be present to consecrate with prayer and the laying on of hands, in accordance with Scripture and the good tradition of the church: "These they set before the apostles, and they prayed and laid their hands on them. And the word of God continued to increase, and the number of the disciples multiplied greatly in Jerusalem, and a great many of the priests became obedient to the faith" (Acts 6:6–7).

People can have minor differences in conception concerning what actually happens during the consecration with the laying on of hands. Some think that it mostly deals with a visible order of symbolic character. Then there are various grades of both the sacramental and charismatic approaches that highlight that it really is something concrete that is mediated and done. Roman Catholics speak about an ontological dimension so that the priest is changed in his essence through ordination. Personally, I find myself somewhere between the symbolic and charismatic. The ordination is an important symbolic event where other offices are present, and the whole congregation gives its recognition to the one who is consecrated. But in light of the Scriptures, it is obvious that something also happens of a deeper and more spiritual dimension. Perhaps a person can describe it as an impartation of a spiritual anointing, a mediation or an awakening of specific charismatic gift for ministry. Here I find support among other places in the words that Paul directed to Timothy: "For this reason I remind you to fan into flame the gift of God, which is in you through the laying on of my hands" (2 Tim. 1:6) and "do not neglect the gift you have, which was given you by prophecy when the council of elders laid their hands on you" (1 Tim. 4:14). There is, however, nothing unambiguously prescribed in the Bible for how this laying on of hands or consecration should be done. But throughout history, the church has developed a tradition and a good order for this, which we do well to follow. There is a hierarchical dimension with bishops who have a central and overall responsibility for leadership. It is a holy order that creates security and unity; this is contrasted with anarchy which leads to chaos and uneasiness.

So, we return to the introduction of this chapter where I described the office from the concepts of authorization, representation, and legitimization. None of us wants to end up on an operation table and be in the hands of a surgeon who lacks medical training and a doctor's license. We also recognize that legal security in society is founded upon us citizens recognizing that we cannot take the law into our own hands and administer justice from our own thoughts. There is an order to society that is for the well-being of citizens. This external societal order is affirmed by the New Testament and considered to be instituted by God (Rom. 13:1–6). Some form of church order is, in the same way, fundamental for the function of the office as well as the unity and prosperity of the church. "For God is not a God of confusion but of peace" (1 Cor. 14:33).

When this order serves the pure proclamation of the gospel and the proper administration of the sacraments and the expansion of God's kingdom, it has many advantages that also recommend it for the future of the church. The reformers recognized this good order of the church and would have rather kept it. But they were forced to break with it when they lost favor with the bishops through the proclamation of the pure gospel. Their situation is described in *The Apology of the Augsburg Confession*, and they have something important to say even to us:

Article Fourteen, in which we say that no one should be allowed to administer the word and the sacraments unless they are duly called, they accept with the proviso that we use canonical ordination. Concerning this subject, we have frequently testified in the assembly that it is our greatest desire to retain the order of the church and the various ranks in the church—even though they were established by human authority. We know that church discipline in the manner described by the ancient canons was instituted by the Fathers for a good and useful purpose. However, the bishops compel our priests either to reject and condemn the kind of doctrine that we have confessed, or by new and unheard cruelty they kill the unfortunate and innocent people. This prevents our priests from acknowledging such bishops. Thus the cruelty of the bishops is the reason for the abolition of canonical order in some places despite our earnest desire to retain it. Let the bishops ask themselves how they will give an answer to God for breaking up the church.

We have clear consciences on this matter since we know that our confession is true, godly and catholic. For this reason, we dare not approve the cruelty of those who persecute this doctrine. We know that exists among those who rightly teach the Word of God and rightly administer the sacraments; it does not exist among those who not only try to destroy the Word of God with their edicts, but who also butcher those who violate them. Moreover, we want to point out again that we would willingly retain ecclesiastical and canonical order as long as the bishops desisted from their cruelty against our churches. This willingness will be our defense, both before God and among all nations, present and future, against the charge that we have undermined the authority of the bishops. Thus people may read and hear that, despite our protest against the unjust cruelty of the bishops, we could obtain no justice.[7]

When bishops refuse to ordain and consecrate those who keep a high view of the Holy Scriptures and boldly preach Christ crucified, then one of the church's highest offices has been kidnapped and abused. There is something above bishops and all offices, despite the foundational good order, and it is the gospel and its pure proclamation. The church stands or falls on this gospel, and, without it, there is no longer anything to administer.

· C H A P T E R   9 ·

Divine Service

Concerning the Form and Formation of the Church

Sixth, the holy Christian people are externally recognized by
prayer, public praise, and thanksgiving to God. Where you
see and hear the Lord's Prayer prayed and taught; or psalms or
other spiritual songs sung, in accordance with the word of God
and the true faith; also the creed, the Ten Commandments, and
the catechism used in public, you may rest assured that a holy
Christian people of God are present. For prayer, too, is one of
the precious holy possessions whereby everything is sanctified,
as St. Paul says [1 Tim. 4:5]. The psalms too are nothing but
prayers in which we praise, thank, and glorify God. The creed
and the Ten Commandments are also God's word and belong to
the holy possession, whereby the Holy Spirit sanctifies the holy
people of Christ. However, we are now speaking of prayers and
songs which are intelligible and from which we can learn and by
means of which we can mend our ways. The clamor of monks
and nuns and priests is not prayer, nor is it praise to God; for
they do not understand it, nor do they learn anything from it;
they do it like a donkey, only for the sake of the belly and not at
all in quest of any reform or sanctification or of the will of God.[1]

O Come Let Us Worship

Man was created to worship. That we worship is then not only something religious and churchly but something deeply human. Worship touches upon the deepest meaning of existence itself; we exist to worship. The question, then, is not if we shall worship, but rather what or whom we shall worship. Here, worship does not mean singing songs or participating in certain religious events, but in what we seek for our deepest satisfaction, comfort, and security. That which is our god is really that which we rely on and from which we expect all good things. Therefore, the first and greatest commandment deals with worship. The whole of creation is created to worship, but it is only the Creator that is worthy of our worship. That God wants to have our confidence and worship is for our best so that our life shall be directed toward and revolve around that which is genuinely good. All that is good and beautiful in creation touches us and can capture our heart, but when we seek our comfort and meaning in created things, our whole life is warped. It is idolatry to make the good gifts of God into the highest good and place our confidence in them. We may appreciate, use, and cultivate creation, but when our appreciation becomes confidence and thereby worship, we have disfigured the true purpose of life. We touch upon this in Luther when in the Large Catechism concerning the First Commandment, he defined what it is to have a God.

> A "god" is the term for that to which we are to look for all good and in which we are to find refuge in all need. Therefore, to have a god is nothing else than to trust and believe in that one with your whole heart. As I have often said, it is the confidence and faith of the heart alone that make both God and an idol . . .

Anything on which your heart relies and depends, I say, that is really your God.[2]

Luther's description of idolatry is deep and rooted in the witness of Scripture. The apostle Paul saw idolatry as the center of sin: a misdirected worship that puts its hope in and seeks its meaning in something other than the Creator:

> For although they knew God, they did not honor him as God or give thanks to him, but they became futile in their thinking, and their foolish hearts were darkened . . . and exchanged the glory of the immortal God for images resembling mortal man and birds and animals and creeping things . . . because they exchanged the truth about God for a lie and worshiped and served the creature rather than the Creator, who is blessed forever! Amen (Rom. 1:21, 23, 25).

Paul's description of man as an idolater refers not only to men in antiquity amidst the decadence of ancient Rome, but it is a description of all men after the fall into sin. We have all made other gods for ourselves next to God and to these we give our love. We put our confidence in them. Luther continued in the Catechism:

> [Y]ou will easily see and judge how the world practices nothing but false worship and idolatry. There has never been a nation so wicked that it did not establish and maintain some sort of worship. All people have set up their own god, to whom they looked for blessings, help, and comfort. [. . .] They all made a god out of what their heart most desired . . . Accordingly the pagans actually fashion their own fancies and dreams about God into an idol and

rely on an empty nothing. So it is with all idolatry. Idolatry does not consist merely of erecting an image and praying to it, but it is primarily a matter of the heart, which fixes its gaze upon other things and seeks help and consolation from creatures, saints or devils. It neither cares for God nor expects good things from him sufficiently to trust that he wants to help, nor does it believe that whatever good it encounters comes from God.[3]

We Become What We Worship

This break with the first commandment leads to our breaking all the other commandments, and on the contrary, "For, said earlier, where the heart is rightly set toward God and this commandment is observed, all the other commandments follow."[4] When something other than God is at the center in our lives, everything else in life ends up in the wrong place. As Paul described it:

> And since they did not see fit to acknowledge God, God gave them up to a debased mind to do what ought not to be done. They were filled with all manner of unrighteousness, evil, covetousness, malice. They are full of envy, murder, strife, deceit, maliciousness. They are gossips, slanderers, haters of God, insolent, haughty, boastful, inventors of evil, disobedient to parents, foolish, faithless, heartless, ruthless. Though they know God's righteous decree that those who practice such things deserve to die, they not only do them but give approval to those who practice them (Rom. 1:28–31).

The prophets of the Old Testament often described idolatry as worthless. And the reason is that it cannot give us what we need (Psalm

115:4–8). Idols never deliver; they are incapable of giving us what we at our deepest level long for most. For this reason, misfortune and worry always follow from idolatry. A common misunderstanding is that idols are religious fantasies or things that are sinful in themselves. But idols in our lives are almost always things that are good in and of themselves, gifts that God has given us but that we abuse. Instead of enjoying them and using them in thankfulness to God, we make them the center about which our lives revolve and give them our hearts. Again, Luther observed:

> It is God alone (as I have repeated often enough) from whom we receive everything good and by whom we are delivered from all evil. [. . .] he [God] is an eternal fountain who overflows with pure goodness and from whom pours forth all that is truly good.
>
> Although much that is good comes to us from human beings, nevertheless, anything received according to his command and ordinance in fact comes from God . . . So we receive our blessings not from them, but from God through them. Creatures are only the hands, channels, and means through which God bestows all blessings. [. . .] Let each and everyone, then, see to it that you esteem this commandment above all things and not make light of it. Search and examine your own heart thoroughly, and you will discover whether or not it clings to God alone. If you have the sort of heart that expects from him nothing but good, especially in distress and need, and renounces and forsakes all that is not God, then you have the one true God. On the contrary, if your heart clings to something else

and expects to receive from it more good and help than from God and does not run to God but flees from him when things go wrong, then you have another god, and idol.[5]

Thus, for Luther, everything depends on the three commandments of the first table, and they affect each other. When one makes his idols equal to God (the first commandment), this results in the misuse of God's name and makes his own false picture of him, which one then prays to (the second commandment). This, in turn, has its basis in that one does not honor the Lord's day and set it apart for divine service where one may listen to God's Word (the third commandment). So, in the other way around, engaging in regular worship is a must if we don't wish to end up as idolaters. But not just any worship service will do, but such as mediates that which we have spoken about in former chapters. The divine service is the place where the true faith is to be proclaimed and mediated, where the people of God are formed and edified. Here, our confidence is established, and our worship is formed. A true worship then is inseparable from the Christian life. As Luther wrote about the third commandment:

> For the Word of God is the true holy object above all holy objects . . . God's Word is the treasure that makes everything holy. By it all the saints have themselves been made holy. At whatever time God's Word is taught, preached, heard, read or pondered, there the person, the day, and the word is hallowed, not on account of the external work but on account of the Word that makes us all saints. Accordingly, I constantly repeat that all our life and work must be based on God's Word if they are to be God-pleasing or holy. Where that happens the

commandment is in force and is fulfilled. [. . .] Note, then, that the power and force of this commandment consists not in the resting but in the hallowing, so that this day may have its special holy function . . . In this case, however, a work must take place through which a person becomes holy. This work, as we have heard, takes place through God's Word. Places, times, persons and the entire outward order of worship have therefore been instituted and appointed in order that God's Word may exert its power publicly.[6]

The Divine Service Is at the Center of a Christian's Life

In the New Testament, there is no Christian faith apart from the life of the church. A person does not become a Christian on a personal level and then decide to join a church if he feels like it. To be a Christian in the New Testament is to be baptized into the body of Christ and become part of the life of the church and her communion. The church administers the Christian faith, and the divine service is the central place where God's Word is proclaimed, the forgiveness of sins is mediated, baptism is performed, and the gifts of the Lord's Supper are distributed. Here, prayers, song, and creedal confessions are said. The divine service is the place where the church comes into being and takes visible shape and from which all else is born, grows, and is formed. Then, our life is placed in the greater context of God's great narrative, which indicates a pattern for faith and everyday life. Comfort is mediated in the divine service. Our faith is formed and given depth by our worship. There, we are also equipped for service, and we are sent out into everyday life in order to spread the gospel and serve our neighbors in the world.

What then characterizes a divine service in this one, holy, catholic and apostolic church? The divine service is the foremost expression of Christian faith and, simultaneously, the instrument God uses to more and more anchor and form our lives in and by this faith. What happens in our worship exposes our theology, how we at the deepest level view and express our faith, how we consider God and his purpose and plan for the world and humanity. We cannot do what we want with the divine service without risking a false witness concerning God. In our day, there is an endless push to experiment with the forms of the divine service, without consideration as to how the container influences the content. Form and content can never really be separated even if many try to claim just that. Certainly, a person can successfully draw more visitors by inventing new forms of worship, but the question is what is really mediated and what sort of Christian is formed when we do it. The great question is therefore not what we should do with the divine service, but what the divine service should do with us.

Words such as "stage," "performance," "production," and "audience" do not belong to the vocabulary of the divine service. God is the primary actor in the divine service, not us. It is his Word and actions that are central, not ours. The focus of the divine service, then, is not our service and our sacrifice before God; it is God who serves us by giving us the sacrifice Jesus fulfilled, through the Word and sacraments. In reformational—or, more specifically, Lutheran—traditions, worship is, as mentioned above, called precisely "The Divine Service." So, there is a focus on what God says and does for us through the Word and the sacraments. God serves us by our serving him. He takes us into his service in order to use our mouths to speak his Word and our hands to give us his gifts. The center of the divine service is Christ's real presence through Word and sacraments, where he comes to us and distributes all his blessings to us. There, we may receive God's promise with our eyes and ears, our hands and our mouths. We see and hear, taste, feel, and smell. When we have received Christ and his blessings, we are sent out to serve in the world to give form to God's Kingdom in many different ways. As the old Swedish archbishop Yngve Brilioth described it:

> In the divine service God deals with his congregation through the word and the holy sacraments. There the congregation also deals with God in a devotional reception, in hymns and prayer. Then the Holy Spirit purifies again, creates a communion of men around the means of grace, and edifies God's church. So the divine service is as inalienable for the church as it is for the individual. No other form of devotion can replace the congregational gathering in God's house.[7]

This is different from how many people think about worship today. For example, there is a trend within nondenominational or independent churches today to look for the spectacular and extraordinary, when it comes to both creativity and technique as well as the spiritual. Church leaders seek new expressions, effective tools, and "customer-friendly" forms for attracting people and mediating the message. This manner of thinking would be completely foreign to the reformers. It was just this, "the medieval show of the mass," that they turned away from and wanted to get rid of in the church. This was the case during the late Middle Ages; preaching had been marginalized, and the administration of the sacraments had come to be conceived as something the priests did in front of the people "for show." In contrast to this, Luther elevated the sermon's central role in the divine service and made the Lord's Supper accessible for all under both elements, that is, offering both the bread and the wine.

The reformers trusted that God carried out his work in men through the means of grace. It may seem remarkable to us modern Christians to depend so much on Word and sacrament, as we are occupied with helping God get moving by constantly offering him new vehicles. But the power of Word and sacrament, and their effectiveness, only depends on him who is active in and through them, namely, God himself through the present Christ by the Holy Spirit. That God works through Word and sacrament in the divine service is completely in line with how God always works in the world. He takes that which is nothing, that which seems to be weak in the world and even foolish, and carries out his powerful work through it, so that man shall not have anything to brag about (1 Cor. 1:27–29). As Luther expressed it: "What God institutes and commands cannot be useless. Rather, it is a most precious thing, even though to all appearances it may not be worth a straw."[8] Paul spoke in the same spirit when he described himself and his proclamation. He presented himself as someone completely different from a self-confident motivational speaker or rhetoric expert, and he does not want to make use of anything to awaken attention or convince anyone other than the pure gospel:

> And I, when I came to you, brothers, did not come proclaiming
> to you the testimony of God with lofty speech or wisdom. For
> I decided to know nothing among you except Jesus Christ and
> him crucified. And I was with you in weakness and in fear and
> much trembling, and my speech and my message were not in

plausible words of wisdom, but in demonstration of the Spirit and of power, so that your faith might not rest in the wisdom of men but in the power of God (1 Cor. 2:1–5).

The Divine Service as Participation

Many think that our society is becoming more individualistic. Everyone wants to do their own thing. Formed by our age, we worship individual freedom and independence. The result has been a lost experience of community and oneness, and a privatization of faith that leads to a separation and isolation. In ecclesiastical contexts, this approach leads to an overemphasis on the personal relationship to God: my private faith and my God, as I understand God, distinct from the church's communion and divine service and without historical roots. It is not seldom that this also leads to the segregation of generations, where preferences and taste divide us into different groups that stand opposed to each other. A distortion of the divine service even happens when it is formed simply from evangelistic or missional ambitions. Even here, a divided existence is created, the picture of wholeness broken, and false dichotomies created. Divine services with so-called low thresholds, "seeker-sensitive," and a relevant talk for the unchurched, ironically enough, create an even more obvious "us and them." The distortion of the divine service can have many different expressions; let us look a little closer at them and what consequences they have.

A divine service that has been disconnected from the common Christian patterns and practices cuts its historical roots and loses its eschatological perspective. When we celebrate the divine service, we do it as a one, holy, catholic, and apostolic church, an unbroken chain through the centuries of worshipers. In the divine service, heaven and earth meet. We celebrate the divine service together with all the heavenly host and all the saints who have gone before us. Here, there is no "us and them." Here, there is only a single "us and Him"; all God's people throughout all times and before God's throne. In the divine service, the church of the past is united with the church of the future in the present. The message and its proclamation are, at its deepest level, timeless. Even the people are timeless in a way. Society develops, the welfare gets better, and trends shift, but the needs and demands of the human soul remain; its questions and struggles are to a large degree the same throughout the whole of history. We can read the *Confessions of Saint Augustine* from the fourth century and recognize ourselves, just as we can recognize ourselves in texts from Homer and Shakespeare. Everything is the same but different circumstances. The environment has changed, but human beings by their nature are the same and continually struggle with the same dilemmas and questions.

A divine service that breaks with the great Christian tradition and experiments with "seeker-friendly" adaptations to the contemporary culture also risks leaving behind the apostolic teaching that is the foundation of the church. Then, the church can be changed into a spiritual shopping center with great and various offerings of all sorts. There are generous open times, great crowds gather, but all are private individuals, customers, who shop according to their own felt needs. Here, there is no friction, nothing to chew on; all is well adapted to our modern tastes. Worship services that get their inspiration from this source hardly come to form people in the likeness of Christ. Rather, one is formed according to narcissistic consumption that grabs for itself from a great smorgasbord of experiences, tips, and bits of advice.

Faith is certainly personal, but it is never individualistic and cannot be reduced to private opinions. The divine service proclaims, manifests, and mediates a foretaste of the kingdom of God that is already present through the church, but which still needs to come in its fullness. With a clear and well thought out liturgy, we are united through the universal words and rituals in prayer, songs, the creeds, and the sacraments. The divine service is, in other words, something completely different from a lecture, a social event, or a concert. Here, we are all invited to partake in the gospel in word and deeds and thereby create a union between us, a oneness that is not found anywhere else in the world. The renewal of the church does not happen by moving away from faith's center, but by a perpetual return to the sources.

A worship service that deviates from the historical pattern also risks creating an unnecessary contradiction by maintaining its unique profile in conflict with the historical and worldwide church. Instead of seeking the center and so confirming the unity we have with Christ's church in Word and the sacraments, in the prayers and the confessions, one risks ending up in extremes and thus dividing the body of Christ. However, the body does not consist of a single part, but of many. The body can live without a limb, but a lone limb dies if it does not sit together with the body. Therefore, the eye cannot say to the hand, "I do not need you" (1 Cor. 12:21). In the liturgy, there is something more than just individual believers; here, we are formed into a people of God and the body of Christ. It creates an active participation of all of us. It is an expression of the unity of the Church, and it strengthens the fellowship of the faith. A liturgy that is well rooted in the church's historical worship tradition signals that there is a continuity and connection with the church throughout all times and throughout the world.

A worship service that leaves behind the universal Christian pattern for worship also risks segregating the generations. When a person reasons from commercial business considerations and works with "target groups," he risks tailoring worship styles for different preferences and tastes, young and old. The elderly are assumed to like some forms and the younger, others; so, a man therefore works with different types of services that should suit different generations. Then, rather than the divine service being something that unites God's people, it becomes an expression of division. Instead of the integrative and boundless communion of the saints, the service has a segregating function. Often, we also have given our children and youth a free pass from the divine service, instead of nurturing them to understand and assimilate the divine service. In our misdirected concern for children, we have created alternative gatherings where both form and content are suitable to the restlessness of children, instead of helping them to concentrate, be still, and behold the glory of God. Obviously, different forms of directed activity are needed for children and youth. Yet, we ought not create assemblies that risk vaccinating them against the possibility of worshiping in ways that are not formed by modern media hype and a high pace. As a twelve-year-old, Jesus took part in the divine service of the temple with great joy and wonder, to the great surprise of his parents. Perhaps even we undervalue the divine service's ability to grab hold of the hearts of children and youth? (Prov. 22:6)

Finally, a divine service that breaks with the historic and universal Christian pattern also risks cementing the categorization of the "us and them," between believers and not-yet believers. When you talk about doing worship services that are completely focused on communicating with non-believers in form and appeal, you make just such a distinction between people. The divine service is then easily conceived of as a type of sales pitch. The appeal distinguishes those who have not yet professed the faith and cements their alienation. But the divine service has a common appeal, timeless but still personal, to all people, both those who believe and those who do not yet believe. Even after we have come to believe in Christ, we are forgiven sinners on the path of change. We all struggle enough with the same problems and carry the same needs in this world, regardless of whether we are Christians or not. The gospel is the only thing that answers life's deepest questions, hurts, and needs. It is the proclamation of the gospel and the mediation of boundless grace that we all need every Sunday. So, before Christ, there is no "us and them," there is only "us and Him."

The Divine Service Forms Faith

In a liturgically rich divine service, faith becomes visible and clear through rituals, signs, and symbols. Such a divine service does not simply direct its message to reason or emotions, but it reaches all senses and involves our whole being, including the body. In his classic book, *Ecclesiastical Renewal* (*Kyrklig förnyelse*), Father Gunnar Rosendal wrote: "You cannot sanctify the soul and let the body be worldly, for no one knows what the border is between body and soul . . . Where one is not a Christian with the body but modestly wants to satisfy himself with a 'spiritual' Christianity, there the whole Christian life is lost."[9] Therefore, it is not unimportant how the divine service is celebrated. It shapes what and how we believe. Often enough, we make ourselves guilty of sending mixed signals in the divine service; what one hears, does, and sees does not really go together. Everything that happens in a divine service actually proclaims a message of some sort, whether it happens through words or actions, symbols, or architecture. Christian faith does not in itself have contempt for either the body or the material and does not represent an abstract spirituality.

God created us in his image, and he created us with a body. Jesus wants not only my heart but my whole being with spirit, body, and soul. We are to love and worship God with our whole heart, the whole of our soul, all our understanding, and our whole body. Therefore, the service also engages the body and speaks not only to our inner being. We lift and fold our hands. We open our lips and raise our voices in prayer, hymns, and creedal confession. We fall on our knees and confess our sins. We get up and walk to the altar. There, we eat and drink at the Lord's table. We baptize the body in water; we lay hands on each other in prayer. Our ears are filled with the gospel in sermon and songs; our eyes are fixed upon the symbols that picture the work of salvation. Our nose is filled with the familiar scent of a sanctuary. The whole of our being is touched by and engaged in worship. We must therefore not let the divine service be limited to cognitive information or emotional inspiration, but let faith take root in the whole body. Paul expressed this in the following way:

> I appeal to you therefore, brothers, by the mercies of God, to present your bodies as a living sacrifice, holy and acceptable to God, which is your spiritual worship (Rom. 12:1).

If we want to be true Christians who live every day by the grace of God and to the glory of God, Sunday must be characterized by a rich celebration of divine service that shapes our whole lives by touching all our senses, instead of being limited to some kind of lecture or performance. The divine service deals with the mediation of the life that proceeds from God in Christ through the Holy Spirit. The divine service must then accommodate and give shape to the three articles of faith: Father, Son, and Spirit. The cross of redemption stands in the center, which is surrounded by the beauty of creation and the Spirit's revelation and stream of life.

The Divine Service That Edifies and Forms

Throughout all of history, God's plan and will has been to create a people who reflect him. The zeitgeist's secular liturgies deform us and lead us astray from God's goal. It shapes us, often on a subconscious level, to seek to embody and reflect alternative and worldly visions of the good life. So, the church's task in the liturgy is to re-form us according to God's plan. This re-formation is a process that forms us over time into the image of Christ. And here, it is obvious that the content cannot be separated from the form. All forms are formative; first we form forms, which in turn form us. Therefore, the question of good theology is intimately connected with the question of good liturgy. A person can learn theology on one level in the classroom, but on a deeper level, a person learns theology in the sanctuary of the church through the liturgy of the divine service. Liturgy is therefore nothing other than theology "in action," embodied and mediated in the divine service. The forms slowly but surely shape our thoughts, hearts, and actions by repetitively communicating God's living and active Word to those of us who participate in the divine service. Yet, it is impossible to get away from the fact that in the divine service we encounter a world that is foreign to us all. The church is an outpost for the kingdom of God. It is in this world but not of it, which means that as an expression of the kingdom of God, the divine service can be experienced as strange and foreign for us. That the church is an outpost for God's kingdom also has consequences for the forms and expressions we choose. It is not just any form and expression that is suitable to give shape to God's kingdom. Consciously or subconsciously, the form of our worship conveys a message that either strengthens or weakens the gospel. The forms we use are therefore never neutral. They carry and mediate a message in themselves and shape us accordingly.

When new visitors experience the divine service as something new and different, it does not have to make us anxious. Then, we might end up in the ditch where we become overly interested in being contextual and adapting the service to the spirit of the times. In our evangelistic zeal, we are then tempted to empty the church of her universal and apostolic essence. By being both biblically and historically anchored, on the other hand, we are tied together as Christians and manifest one holy, catholic, and apostolic church, regardless of tradition or era. We thereby faithfully witness to Christ before the world. The divine service ought to then be marked by a foundational pattern that can be recognized and conceived of as Christian and ecclesiastical throughout the world and which shows a continuity with the church throughout all of history. This pattern has some distinct and indispensable elements. God gathers his people, he speaks to us, comes to us, and sends us back out into the world. We give response in prayer, worship, creedal confession, and by receiving the sacraments. All are partakers, none are spectators. Therefore, the liturgy ought not to be centered on a program performed by professional people on a platform. There is certainly no detailed description in the Bible of exactly how we shall celebrate the divine service nor a total uniformity in how it was formed and celebrated throughout the history of the church. However, there are several central elements that have accompanied the divine service since the church's earliest history, as well as obvious instructions in Scripture about what Christian worship ought to contain, convey, and point to in order to be called Christian.

All sincere Christians are deeply aware that we are not yet quite what we ought to be. We continually struggle with misdirected desires, with thought patterns and actions that are not in harmony with the faith that we confess. However, when we come to the divine service, we submit ourselves to the forms of the liturgy and allow ourselves to be shaped by the actions we do, the words we hear, the prayers we pray, and all that we see. In the words of Aristotle: "We become what we regularly do" or in Augustine's Christian paraphrase: "We become what we worship." In the divine service, we learn both a language and a pattern for our faith. Therefore, what takes place on Sunday is connected to what then happens in everyday life. If, in the divine service, we are merely passive consumers that are offered entertainment and exciting lectures, it does not come to form us into anything but consumers of amusement who day after day seek something that can cure our boredom. As the divine service is, therefore, our Christian life will be, and what the divine service expresses will be reflected in our lives. In short: what happens on Sunday will over time be manifested on Monday.

Someone has said: "As one prays, so one believes, and the converse: as one believes, so one prays." And there is a lot of truth in those words. They illuminate the intimate relationship between form and content, between liturgy and theology. Really, all worship has a certain form, even in the traditions where one makes a big number about being totally free from any kind of form. But where the common Christian liturgy (as it is celebrated according to its main content, by all, always and everywhere) is despised, there the theology will soon be lost as well. The historical liturgical forms are carefully thought through to carry us and root us into the whole biblical story of salvation.

And here there is a great wisdom. The gospel is not so easily lost in an order of worship that always includes the confession of sins, absolution, and the celebration of the Lord's Supper. At their core, such elements and actions are a confession of the most central thing in the gospel. As Berth Löndahl has so wisely pointed out: the universal

Christian liturgy "doubtless has a future for the simple reason that it has a past. Almost two thousand years of the same basic pattern is a tangible testimony . . . only for the reason that it does not only live in time but also from eternity."[10] When Sunday after Sunday, we pray, read, and expound the Holy Scriptures in a form that has its roots in the divine service of the synagogue (Luke 4:16–21), this is a form that has preserved God's Word among us throughout the history of the church. We will allow Giertz to summarize these thoughts:

> There can be no normal congregational life without liturgy. The sacraments need form, the divine service must be held in some manner. It is possible to live for a short time off of improvisations and forms that constantly develop and are recreated. One can pray free prayers, and create a new ritual for every worship occasion. But the possibilities are soon exhausted. One has to repeat and so the formation of rituals is in full swing. In circles where one attempts to live without any forms, a new form is always made. Favorite songs return repeatedly, there are certain turns in prayer that are constantly repeated, and there are firmly fixed annual traditions with certain traditional ceremonies. And it is no injustice to say that the new forms that grow out of this manner are uglier and more profane than the old liturgy. Their contents have less of God's word, they do not pray and talk with scriptural inference, they are not anxious to bring forth the entire council of Scripture, but are satisfied with one and another that seem particularly striking or popular. The new liturgy, that comes about in this way, is poorer, less biblical and less nourishing for the soul than the old that one had before.[11]

The Divine Service as Repetition and Ritual

When frustration over unsatisfactory results grips us, we are reminded of our era's restlessness and rootlessness. We are then tempted to abandon the proven pattern that has carried the faith through the centuries, in order to win short-term victories. An obvious temptation is to seek success through great crowds and popularity. Then, the Christian divine service is evaluated by its entertainment and experiential value rather than from its unique ability to reveal and equip us with the truth. Within independent churches, life and inspiration are often emphasized at the expense of learning and formation. Repetition and ritual, which some consider to be mechanical and monotonous, are downplayed to the benefit of spontaneity. However, all human learning and teaching has within it an element of repetition, and if we want to form disciples in the image of Christ, repetition ought to be a part of our worship. Over and over again, the same thing, until it is in the bones.

The divine service can and should contain certain variations, but not at the expense of the power that is found in the repetition of the faith's central truths. It is with the divine service as it is with life in general. It is the routines, the things that we repeat time after time, that form us into who we are. Through the repetition of certain moments, knowledge and skill become an integrated part of our person. It is not always that we think about what we do or experience something special when we carry out our routines. But this is exactly what routine actions are about, not letting our lives be left to the whim of the moment or occasional desire. Someone has said it this way: "I have brushed my teeth ten thousand times, sometimes more asleep than awake. Most often it happens without any major experience, but I know that, despite this, every occasion had effect and contributed to a great result, in the hour of testing at the yearly dental checkup." There is a risk that we miss the long-term perspective when we constantly want to evaluate ourselves. The result of what our divine services can accomplish cannot be measured already on Sunday evening, but perhaps can rightly be judged from what type of faith it forms in the long run in the regular worshiper.

Sugar-sweet events can perhaps give immediate and great effects, but they are usually shortsighted. On the other hand, a nutritional divine service, filled with the riches of the Christian faith, can be difficult to absorb at the beginning. A little austere in its design, it has little appeal for the consumer of entertainment. But it is durable. It has remained through all the changes of the centuries and has helped the church to rejoice and grow in the faith. At first glance, a divine service that follows an historical liturgical pattern may be experienced as both unattractive and inaccessible to a modern person, but it has a remarkable ability to meet our deepest needs if we give it some time. In our incredibly individualistic world where we are slaves to our subjective feelings and thinking, it is a great relief to subordinate ourselves to the divine service's stable and measured form. It is liberating to be able to follow a finished pattern that gently and steadily leads us through the various parts of the divine service. Instead of carrying the service ourselves, we get to experience being carried by it. The divine service then becomes a liberated zone, instead of yet another arena for further accomplishment and self-realization.

The Divine Service as Proclamation of the Gospel

That God has reconciled us to himself in Christ Jesus—by grace alone, through faith alone—is our central message, our most important article of faith upon which the whole existence of the church rests. Take away the gospel, and everything is lost. What is unique about the church is really not her ethics, but the gospel. It is the church's highest and most holy treasure which we are set to administer and proclaim. Only the church possesses this message, and this is God's power for salvation for whoever believes. So, we proclaim the gospel as God's answer to the most fundamental problem of the world and man, in every part of the divine services. If the gospel goes silent in the churches, there is no one else to preach it. However, we have the promise of Jesus that the stones will begin to cry out if this happens. And surely in our day, one can now and then hear the "stones" cry out, while the church is surprisingly silent concerning that which is unfortunately her best-kept secret. Certainly, the church's message and forms can, in comparison with contemporary slogans and cultural expression, seem hopelessly old fashioned and irrelevant. But in the deepest sense, the question of the divine service is about our confidence that the gospel actually has the power to do and deliver what it promises. When we lose faith in that power, updating our forms of communication and worship seems like a good solution. However, when we get renewed confidence in the gospel and its effect to change the life of men, we think differently. This is not the least apparent in the form and structure of the divine service.

Even if the liturgy is very important, it is then not an end in and of itself; its task is only to point to and mediate the gospel to us. Liturgy is important only because the gospel is important. The various parts of the divine liturgy ought in themselves be a proclamation of the gospel from beginning to the end. The liturgy narrates and anchors us in the great biblical narrative of creation, fall, redemption, and renewal. Even if the divine service looks different in different traditions during the church's history, there is a pattern and a structure (ordo) that has been agreed upon in principle everywhere. Its elements are: Gathering—Word—Table—Sending. God calls and gathers us to worship before his face. God speaks his Word to us and through the proclamation of the Word, awakens faith and new life in us. God invites us to his table, and in faith we receive his gifts and are united through the bread and wine into one body and one people. God again sends us out into the world in service to our neighbor. All this is nothing but gospel in word and deed. God calls. God speaks. God gives. God sends. We come. We worship. We receive. We go.

Without a liturgy that follows the biblical and evangelical pattern, the entire worship service lies in the hands of the pastor. The risk then is that everything is characterized by the pastor's personality and matters of his heart—or that which seems to give quick results. Without the good liturgy, the pastor can also be tempted to give in to what strong people in the congregation prefer or be driven by his own thirst for approval and praise. But through a liturgy that is built around the great biblical narrative and the story of salvation, every moment of the service is permeated by the gospel. When every part of the divine service is well-anchored and formed by God's Word, it shields us from occupying ourselves with something other than the gospel. To end this chapter in a rather blunt way, and yet simultaneously pushing one of the benefits concerning our topic: the divine liturgy protects the congregation from the pastor and the pastor from the congregation.

The Cross

Concerning the Life and Commission of the Church in the World

Seventh, the holy Christian people are externally recognized
by the holy possession of the sacred cross. They must endure
every misfortune and persecution, all kinds of trials and evil
from the devil the world and the flesh (as the Lord's Prayer
indicates) by inward sadness, timidity, fear, outward poverty,
contempt, illness, and weakness, in order to become like their
head, Christ. And the only reason they must suffer is that they
steadfastly adhere to Christ and God's word, enduring this for
the sake of Christ, Matthew 5 [:11], "Blessed are you when men
persecute you on my account." [. . .] And all of this is done not
because they are adulterers, murderers, thieves, or rogues,
but because they want to have none but Christ, and no other
God. Wherever you see or hear this, you may know that the
holy Christian church is there, as Christ says in Matthew 5
[:11–12], "Blessed are you when men revile you and utter all
kinds of evil against you on my account. Rejoice and be glad,
for your reward is great in heaven." This too is a holy possession
whereby the Holy Spirit not only sanctifies his people, but also
blesses them.[1]

The Sending from the Worship to the World, from Sunday to Monday, from the Sanctuary to the Streets

We have now come to the last chapter in this book, and it will fit well as a dismissal for sending us out into God's mission in the world. In the preceding chapters, I have focused on what Christ's church is and through what means God carries out his work in us. In this concluding chapter, we will focus on what God does in the world through the church, thus our commission. The place of the Christian church and Christian people is really in the midst of the world. The call, or the sending, is not to flee from the world but to be found in the midst of society, in the family, in the neighborhoods, in schools and places of work, and to be a witness to Christ right there and then. Therefore, the church cannot distance itself from the world, but neither can she allow herself to be adapted to the spirit of the age. Instead, we should allow ourselves to be transformed through the renewal of the mind (Rom. 12:2) so that we become useful in the world. The church's call can briefly be described with the words of Jesus to be the light and salt of the earth (Matt. 5:13–14). On the way to the cross, Jesus prays for his disciples: "I have given them your word, and the world has hated them because they are not of the world, just as I am not of the world. I do not ask that you take them out of the world, but that you keep them from the evil one. They are not of the world, just as I am not of the world. Sanctify them in the truth; your word is truth. As you sent me into the world, so I have sent them into the world" (John 17:14–18). This paradoxical relationship to the world, being in it but not of it, inevitably creates tension and sometimes also conflicts and persecution. All people encounter problems and opposition of different types, but the church encounters a very special type of suffering that follows on her confession of Jesus Christ as Lord (Matt. 10:38).

Persecution can take different forms, from suspicion and marginalization to violence and martyrdom. The temptation to compromise with the world in order to escape suffering is therefore always present. Longing after the acceptance and confirmation from the world can make the church like the insecure teenager in the schoolyard whose highest desire is to be a part of the popular "in crowd" and is therefore willing to play along if she can join the gang. But, as Jesus points out, if the salt loses its saltiness, then what's the use of the salt? Suffering and persecution have been a part of the church's experience throughout its history. However, this has not been wholly negative. The fact is that the church has often been at her best when it has been the most questioned and attacked. On the other hand, when the church has begun to mingle in the corridors of power, she has often become an easy prey for various temptations. Drunk on the world's attention, her identity has been deformed and her God-given commission forgotten. When the church begins to live for the world's confirmation, it is always the cross that is the first thing to be renegotiated. The cross is and remains a shameful symbol in this world, but a Christendom without the cross is a Christendom without power and without Christ. Cross-less Christianity sees Jesus as an example to follow rather than a savior to receive. However, when we trade away the cross, suffering, and death for the benefit of common humanism, and focus only on the fight for social justice, we simultaneously turn away from God's salvific actions and lose the power and life of the resurrection.

Crux sola est nostra theologia. This famous Latin slogan was coined by Luther and is translated into English as: "The cross alone is our theology."

A bold proclamation that has been provocative throughout the ages, particularly to those who want to make Christendom simply into a moral code. Central to Luther's thinking is the theology of the cross, *theologia crucis*. One may then not limit it to a mere teaching about the Atonement; for Luther, the cross is the lens through which everything is viewed. Like an icon, the cross is not only an object we shall look at, but an interpretative screen through which the whole of our existence can be understood. The cross and suffering are the places where God reveals himself most starkly, and it is a pattern for how God works in history and in the world, often in weakness. It remains hidden for those who seek God in the spectacular. How, then, is the Christian life and the church shaped when it is characterized by the cross? How do we perceive our mission and our discipleship in light of the cross? How do we measure success and adversity, strength and weakness if it is observed through the lens of the cross? I will discuss these questions in the remainder of this chapter.

To Take Up Your Cross Is to Live Every Day in Your Baptism

And calling the crowd to him with his disciples, he said to them, "If anyone would come after me, let him deny himself and take up his cross and follow me. For whoever would save his life will lose it, but whoever loses his life for my sake and the gospel's will save it. For what does it profit a man to gain the whole world and forfeit his soul? For what can a man give in return for his soul? For whoever is ashamed of me and of my words in this adulterous and sinful generation, of him will the Son of Man also be ashamed when he comes in the glory of his Father with the holy angels" (Mark 8:34–38).

The Christians in Rome, to whom the evangelist Mark originally wrote, knew very well what it meant to take up their cross. Crucifixion was a brutal and relatively common form of execution that the Roman authorities used. It was meant for grave criminals and those who stood up to the Caesar, but after a while, the Christians were considered to be in this category. Those sentenced to death by crucifixion had to carry their cross to the place of execution as a public recognition of their crime and subjection to the sentence. Yet God changed the symbol of the cross and gave it new meaning through the work of Christ. The cross stands for both death and resurrection, the end of the old creation and the beginning of the new. The Christian encounters death and resurrection in baptism. In this meaning, baptism is our cross. Therefore, in the deepest sense, to "take up your cross" means to live every day in your baptism, dead to the old life and living through Christ. Through baptism, we are included in Christ; we are united with him in his death and resurrection (Rom. 6). So, sanctification and discipleship mean nothing more than to be that which we already are through baptism, dead to sin and alive to Christ.

I briefly discussed the meaning of baptism in the chapter on baptism, but baptism's basic motif has good reason to be repeated. Baptism happens only once, but its reality needs to be perceived and applied daily. The salvation that God bestows in baptism is not completed until Christ raises us up on the last day to live with him in the new creation, but the completion of this salvation is predetermined in baptism with a promise. Under the water, our bodies are immersed in death, to then be raised up with Christ in the new life of resurrection. In a sense, then, death is not ahead of the baptized but behind him. Because in baptism we have already died with Christ, we no longer need to fear death. "For through the law I died to the law, so that I might live to God. I have been crucified with Christ. It is no longer I who live, but Christ who lives in me. And the life I now live in the flesh I live by faith in the Son of God, who loved me and gave himself for me," as Paul wrote in Galatians 2:19–20.

It is Christ's love that drives the Christian. This is a generous love that always seeks the best for his neighbor. It is the way of the cross. Now I no longer live for myself; Christ takes form in me for the sake of my neighbor. Paul formulated this truth in a challenging way. "For the love of Christ controls us, because we have concluded this: that one has died for all, therefore all have died; and he died for all, that those who live might no longer live for themselves but for him who for their sake died and was raised" (2 Cor. 5:14–15). This is the great challenge of the church in all times, that every day we take up our cross, crucify the old man with his demands, and live in the reality of baptism.

To Take Up Your Cross Means to Live in Your Vocation

Each one should remain in the condition in which he was called. Were you a bondservant when called? Do not be concerned about it. (But if you can gain your freedom, avail yourself of the opportunity.) For he who was called in the Lord as a bond-servant is a freedman of the Lord. Likewise he who was free when called is a bondservant of Christ. You were bought with a price; do not become bondservants of men. So, brothers, in whatever condition each was called, there let him remain with God (1 Cor. 7:20–24).

One of the most important contributions of the Reformation to the church is that which came to be called the doctrine of vocation. In the middle ages, it was thought that vocation with a capital V was reserved for those who served within the church or the cloister, meaning priests, monks, and nuns. If someone wanted to serve God with real dedication, this could not happen within the sphere of a normal family or gainful employment; they had to go to the monastery. Luther revealed the flaws and limitations that hid themselves behind these pious thoughts, and he elevated the mother's care for children, the farmer's work with his land, and similar human endeavors above the monk's self-imposed asceticism. Thus, to serve God and give him glory does not just concern traditional worship and prayer, but also includes your work life, family, and everyday chores that in various ways are a service to the neighbor.

So, the cross we have to bear as Christians is not something we ourselves have sought and laid upon ourselves, but is found in everyday tasks and responsibilities. It is called a cross precisely because it is not self-imposed. Life offers us many opportunities to serve where patience and love for the neighbor are tested. There are many opportunities for generous love, but also occasions to chasten and crucify one's own flesh. So, to live in service for your neighbor in everyday life should not be considered as something lowly that we ought to avoid in favor of private spiritual exercises. It is the arena for our vocation and discipleship, and a means for our sanctification. The Lutheran doctrine of vocation has upgraded daily tasks and made the whole of life into a divine service. Unfortunately, the expression "Protestant Work Ethic" has often found a false meaning and is likened to a joyless experience where we toil to show ourselves worthy to God. To be a moral citizen and manage a work life is then not a good deed through which we are accepted by God. God does not give us the forgiveness of sins as a reward for something we have done; he gives it as a gift, freely and for nothing. It is because we have already been accepted and justified by grace alone that we have been freed to serve our neighbor. So, in Christ, our entire everyday life is drawn into God's operation so that God's kingdom can take form in the world. Therefore, work and family life in the home are just as important in God's eyes as prayer and worship in the sanctuary. That God then calls certain people to serve in his church, for example, as priests, pastors, or deacons is something great and wonderful, but this service deals with "equipping the saints to carry out their ministry" (Eph. 4:12); therefore, these servants should not be regarded as Christian superheroes who have a special relationship to God on the basis of their ministry. All ministers are chief servants and are there only to serve the saints so they in their turn can be fully engaged in their respective vocations.

From a missional perspective, perhaps our greatest challenge lies right here, on the level of everyday life. The church has all too often bought into the lie that "we do not reach out." One often hears proclamations accusing people of this. Then a person thinks about the church's commission from a certain conception of evangelization where the gospel reaches people through campaigns and punctual events. However, the truth is that through her members the church touches innumerable people outside the church every day, just where they are in everyday life, in school, at work, and in various recreational activities. Christ's church is therefore not recognized as a people who look down on the "worldly" and who strive after a "spiritual" existence.

With joy and vocational certainty, the Christian takes on the smallest and most common tasks because they are given from God's hands.

To Take Up Your Cross Means to Travel the Path of the Cross

The hymn of Christ found in the second chapter of Philippians concerning the humiliation and emptying of Christ that led to God's exaltation of him stands in stark contrast to the first Adam's self-exaltation that led to the fall. The Old Adam who lives within us ever since the day of the fall constantly wants to rise up, while Christ's pattern of movement is always downward. Christ's descent is also the path for his holy church. The cross, in this sense, always stands in contrast to the human cultures that are characterized by seeking after strength and glory. Different forms of cultural Christianity emphasize the politically correct and that which is suitable for the occasion, rather than the foolishness of the cross. Strength then takes precedence over weakness, achievements and grand results over faithfulness, popularity before loyalty to Christ and the gospel. The pattern of the cross radically breaks with all human notions of how God works and acts, where strength and success are always considered as that worth striving for. But God paradoxically reveals himself, above all, in the small and the weak, not in the great and strong. This pattern was most clearly demonstrated in the birth, life, and death of Jesus. Christ came to earth as an infant, fully human with all the needs and concerns that a child has. God did not come into the world to join the stars in the palace, but he was born in a simple stable among lowly shepherds and animals. This pattern characterizes everything in Christ's life, from the crib to the cross, God's glory is hidden behind flesh and blood.

This is how God continues to work in and through the church. Through what is little, weak, and seemingly foolish. But the zeitgeist constantly awakens the old man's natural inclination to the great, strong, and spectacular. There is today a widespread cult within the church that puts "the seekers" at the center rather than the gospel of Christ. We are more concerned with making the message relevant for the contemporary culture than that the gospel of Jesus Christ should be heard loud and clear. We are striving to make the church look and sound updated to fit the present. Popular TV programs, entertainment events, night clubs, and rock concerts seem to be the new go-to format when worship services are redesigned. Cool seems to have priority over content, where crowds are valued higher than the Cross of Christ. It is all about whatever draws people in; size and numbers are what counts. It is thought that in order to get people to come to church, we need to get rid of forms and content that may feel old-fashioned, strange, or offensive. This way of thinking is not a modern phenomenon. Paul himself pointed out: "For Jews demand signs and Greeks seek wisdom, but we preach Christ crucified, a stumbling block to Jews and folly to Gentiles" (1 Cor. 1:22–23). Christ comes to us through the Word, and in the water, and in the bread and the wine. Baptism in the water is not exactly a spectacular rite. The Lord's Supper consists of simple bread and wine. This is how God has chosen to mediate his grace to us, in the simple and lowly. Faith itself is mediated to us through the Word of the gospel in simple sentences and statements. Yet through these humble means, Christ himself comes to us. This is how God has chosen to operate. Christ's church is therefore recognized in a strength that is revealed in weakness, a wisdom that appears as foolishness, and where the greatness is found in the small, simple, and often fragile vessels of this world.

Rediscovering the Theology of the Cross

> We are afflicted in every way, but not crushed; perplexed, but
> not driven to despair; persecuted, but not forsaken; struck
> down, but not destroyed; always carrying in the body the death
> of Jesus, so that the life of Jesus may also be manifested in our
> bodies. For we who live are always being given over to death
> for Jesus' sake, so that the life of Jesus also may be manifested
> in our mortal flesh. So death is at work in us, but life in you
> (2 Cor. 4:8–12).

In the above citation, Paul recounted that which characterized his
apostolic ministry. He presented a theology of the cross that is completely contrary to all forms of theology of success. It could rather be
compared to a theology of failure. It elevates the fragile and weak,
suffering and humiliation as the ways in which God reveals himself
and is active. The church was born amidst persecution and grew with
martyrdom. If we as the church estrange ourselves from our insulted
and persecuted siblings—locally, nationally, and globally—we have
at the same moment distanced ourselves from our Lord and denied
our own identity and history. We need to celebrate and constantly
be reminded of the church's martyrs, but at the same time, let us be
careful not to inflate those celebrations, not to obscure the bloody
brutality concerning what it meant to finish one's days as a Christian
witness on a bonfire, on a cross, or among the beasts in the colosseum.
Underneath it all, the fact that the church's persecution in Western
society today is not worth mentioning is perhaps because the sting of
the cross has been blunted in the church's confession and preaching.
Christ was crucified because of his claim to be the Son of God, his

sharp word concerning man's condition, and his declaration that he himself was man's only hope and salvation. The persecuted church suffers today in the same way on the basis of its uncompromised proclamation concerning Jesus as the savior and as the way, the truth, and the life. Certainly, the church can rightly be criticized for things it does and says because of human flaws and stupidity, but as a rule, persecution is an acknowledgement of the church's faithfulness to the gospel. Christ's church is recognized by the fact that the devil rages against her, that the world persecutes her, and that all human flesh offers her resistance.

Recapturing the Message of the Cross

Unfortunately, the gospel is still the church's best-kept secret. The cross is the message of both God's judgment and God's grace. The work that the Spirit does in a true proclamation of law and gospel can be summarized in the words of Hanna's hymn of praise: "The LORD kills and brings to life;/ he brings down to Sheol and raises up./ The LORD makes poor and makes rich;/ he brings low and he exalts./ He raises up the poor from the dust" (1 Sam. 2:6–8). Law without the gospel leaves us hopeless. It demands what we are incapable of. The gospel without the law makes us indifferent. It speaks about a comfort and relief we do not feel the need for. An improper blending of law and gospel causes both the law's demands and the gospel's promise to be lost.

The two rough beams of the cross proclaim law and gospel. The cross is God's condemnation of sin. It reminds us of sin's appalling consequences and that it was my sin that crucified Christ. Therefore, the cross speaks about God's holiness and his wrath over sin. We cannot truly understand what the cross means for us before we understand that the cross was hoisted up because of us. At the foot of the cross, we all stand condemned, but the condemnation fell on another. God's Son took our place and fulfilled all that needed to be fulfilled in our place. Christ crucified is absolutely central for a true proclamation of the gospel. God's salvation must respond to man's deepest problem. What then is this problem and how is it eliminated? As sinners, we stand as transgressors before God, under the law's condemnation and curse, in short, under God's wrath.

Some maintain that the vicarious suffering of Christ presents the Trinity as some sort of dysfunctional family with a violent father who makes himself guilty of cosmic child abuse. According to this thought, there is in Christ's vicarious suffering on the cross a remarkably horrible image of God that ought to be done away with. But wrath is not a characteristic of God, but God's reaction to sin and evil. Jesus died not so that God should be able to love us, but because God loves us (Rom. 5:8). The New Testament presentation of man as a lost sinner does not reduce in any way our worth as image bearers of God and as God's beloved. That God so greatly loved the world that he gave his only Son for us shows just how tremendously prized we are in God's eyes. Of his own free will, Jesus took on the task to eliminate sin, the punishment and death for the sake of those beloved by God. We cannot evaluate this work with our own measuring stick. When we do this, it testifies to a superficial consideration of Christ's atoning work, something that always leads to the simultaneous loss of the gospel's good news. We may very simply find that the Bible speaks abundantly about sacrifice, blood, vicarious suffering, and death for the sake of man's salvation—and not only find this as a fact, but greatly rejoice in this message of atonement for us. The Bible is not a handbook for life with tips from the coach. It is the story of God's love, which through a bloody settlement with sin makes all the difference between life and death, anxiety and peace, condemnation and acquittal. Christ's church is recognized in the proclamation of Christ and him crucified for us. This stands at the very center of our faith, doctrine, and life. Christ's church is therefore the communion of saints who gather around the pure proclamation of the gospel and the proper administration of the sacraments.

The Church I See

Concerning the Church of the Future and the Future of the Church

In this book, I have wanted to share a vision of what characterizes a reformational church in our day. It is influenced by the
journey I myself have made and the development we saw over
the last decade in the congregation where I served as a pastor—a
Neo-Pentecostal church with a vibrant style full of young adults,
which today operates in the Evangelical-Lutheran Church.
Despite a relatively and publicly recognized success, something
serious was missing, and we found ourselves at a dead end.
During our desperate search for both stability and sustainability,
deeper roots and a clearer center, I wrote down some lines for
myself of what I was looking for. I will let them summarize the
contents of this book. It's the kind of vision I see for the church.
To quote John Lennon: "You may say I'm a dreamer, but I'm not
the only one. I hope someday you'll join us."[1]

Everything Belongs to Us

The church's reformation and the evangelization of the world. The mystery of faith and God's manifested majesty. Creation's beauty and the Spirit's anointing. The preaching of bold proclamation concerning the blood of atonement and the deepening and defense of the faith. Reflection without losing passion. Sacramental mediation and spiritual renewal. Charismatic without becoming fanatic. These are bold visions for the church of the future, carried and nourished by deep roots in the historical church. A church that prioritizes both the missional and diaconal, with a focus on both winning souls and caring for souls. We need a good structure that gives space for both flexibility and order, both form and freedom. A church that affirms both contemplation and action, retreats and advances, that seeks holiness and cultivates devotion. A church that preaches both God's law and God's gospel, and a faith that is active through love and good deeds. We may be both academic and charismatic without conflict between the theological and the practical; we emphasize both doctrine and life. Here, a person can be both intellectual and spiritual. Here, there is room for both the human and the divine, the earthly and the heavenly, for suffering and healing. God's Word is proclaimed, and God's power is demonstrated. Here, both prophets and apologists act. We lift our hands in praise and stretch the same hands out in care for the poor and suffering, the sore and wounded. The cross is our sign of victory—where God and man, heaven and earth, the vertical and the horizontal perspectives are reconciled. "For from him and through him and to him are all things" (Rom. 11:36).

The Church I Need

What then is it I seek in the church? What sort of worship do I need? One that is filled with entertainment, that amuses me and offers an opportunity to escape from everyday struggle and bring some excitement to my otherwise sadly humdrum life? Or do I perhaps need a worship service that preaches the secular vision of the good life and gives me a lecture on the divine shortcuts that will get me there quickly? The deceptive liturgies of this world have already kneaded in its message concerning the freedom of self-fulfillment in the whole of my being. Beautiful beats and sensual imagery have captured and seduced me. Life's deepest meaning and highest goal have been distorted and decimated; now everything revolves around the trinity of self—me, myself and I. The temptation is old, but the wrapping is new: "Certainly, you will not die, you shall become like God!" as creation's first prosperity preacher hissed.

But I do not need one more "jesusfied" Ted talk or pep talk trying to push my performance to succeed in my innumerable attempts at self-fulfillment. Nor do I need more places where I can go to be distracted and forget all of life's distortions. What I need instead is a sacred place where form, tempo, and volume are left untouched by this world's hype and hum. I need a place with a crack where the light from another world gracefully exposes the restlessness of my heart and where I am forced to contemplate the utter vanity of my super-paced life, a place where the lies about myself can be painfully debunked because it is badly needed. I need truth and grace, law and gospel that make me free to see my life for what it really is, so that I can finally quit running and surrender in my attempts to hide from God. I need to recognize that my real problem is within and not outside of me. I need help. *I need a Savior.* I do not need a spiritual coach, a motivational guru, and a do-it-yourself plan. Self-help strategies and religious sentiments are not sufficient to save me from the world's seductive temptations, my own misdirected desires, and the false fairytales that I am all too good at telling myself.

I need something other than political correctness and lukewarm tolerance. I need to hear what a person cannot hear anywhere else—the good gospel that says that all that needs to be done is done already, that the demands that weigh on my shoulders have already been fulfilled by another. I need to be assured that God is gracious and good, that he forgives and helps me precisely where I am in life. So spare me both lectures and performances; I seek the fountain that overflows of grace. I am not in need of information but absolution – not only dogma about stuff, but the delivery of the goods. Let my ears hear, but even my eyes see, my hands touch and receive, my nose smell, and my tongue taste. Give me the rituals that carry me when words fail me. A universal language without voice that makes a statement in silence. Bowed knees and raised hands. The sign of the cross. The water of baptism, the bread and wine of holy communion. The prayers, the texts, and the tones that lift my eyes from self-occupation and navel-gazing, to the glory and greatness of God. Not the hyped-up proclamation songs that tell God what I should do for him, but sensible crafted songs and hymns that declare who he is and what he has done for me.

I need to be reminded that I am all too simply imprisoned by this world's alternative message concerning the good life. I need to see over and over again that I am created to find my greatest joy, highest meaning, and deepest comfort in God alone. I need to be filled and strengthened by the Spirit so I can get over myself and live the new life in Christ, in the middle of a fraudulent world, and despite my innate and indwelling inclination to sin. I need the power to live in grace and to show grace to those who struggle alongside me. My heart is uneasy and restless; only in God does my soul find peace. God, come to my rescue. Lord, hasten to help me. Glory be to the Father and to the Son and to the Holy Spirit, now and forever and ever. Amen. Hallelujah!

Notes

Prelude

1. Philip Melanchthon, *Apology to the Augsburg Confession* (Hereafter ACA) Article 7&8:5,30–32, The Book of Concord, Robert Kolb/Timothy Wengert (Hereafter Kolb/Wengert) (Minneapolis; Fortress Press,2000), 174, 179.

2. The original meaning of catholic is universal; here it is not a reference to the Roman Catholic denomination, which is sometimes referred to as Catholic with a capital C, but is used to show that the church is found across denominational lines.

3. Martin Luther, "On the Councils and the Church." *Luther's Works*, American Edition (from here on AE) Vol. 41 (Philadelphia, Fortress Press, 1966), 148.

4. Olofsson (2015), 268.

5. From my own perspective, I reproduce to a great degree the vision of the church as it was described by Giertz in the books *Christ's Church* (1939), *Church Piety* (1939), and a *Shepherd's Letter to the Diocese of Gothenburg* (1949).

6. Martin Luther, AE Vol. 31, 17.

7. Löwegren (2015).

8. Kolb/Wengert, *The Augsburg Confession*, 43.

Chapter 1

1. Nathan Söderblom (1866-1931) was an influential Swedish clergyman and Archbishop of Uppsala from 1914 to 1931. He was very active in the Ecumenical Movement, both within the Lutheran World and the broader

Christian community. Many of his theological books are highly regarded for their scholarship.

2. Johann Gerhard (1582-1637) was a Lutheran pastor and scholar of the second generation of Lutherans. He is known for his systemization of Lutheran Theology relying on the scholastic method. His works have influenced all successive generations of Lutheran pastors in one way or another.

3. Carl Axel Aurelius Till mötes—herdabrev till Göteborgs stift, (Stockholm, Verbum, 2004), 117–18.

4. St. Ignatius of Antioch, letter to Smyrna 8–9, https://www.order ofstignatius.org/files/Letters/Ignatius_to_Smyrnaeans.pdf March 18th 2019.

5. Cyril, cited in Bo Giertz, *Christ's Church*, translated by Hans Andrae, Kindle version (Eugene, Resource Publications, 2010) loc. 1700–1710.

6. Kolb/Wengert, *Augsburg Confession*, 59, 61, and 105.

7. Giertz, *Christ's Church*, loc. 1885.

8. Mikael Löwegren, *Från konflikt till gemenskap*, (Skellefteå, Artos; 2015), 18.

9. Peter Halldorf, *Att älska sin nästas kyrka som sin egen* (Skellefteå, Artos; 2016), 23.

10. Giertz, *Christ's Church*, loc. 2166, 2189.

11. Gustaf Aulén, *Evangeliskt och romerskt*, (Stockholm, Sveriges kristliga studentrörelse; 1922), 103.

12. Giertz, *Christ's Church*, loc. 2307.

13. Ibid, loc. 2320.

14. Cited by Peter Halldorf (2016), 23.

15. Gunnar Rosendal, *Vårt katolska arv*, (Lund, Geerups; 1956), 7.

16. Halldorf, http://ekumeniskakommuniteten.se/fastebloggen /2016/05/31/djupt-traditionell/ (Hämtad 2017-04-10).

17. Ulrik Josefsson, "Pingstvänner I Svenska kyrkan: pentekostal ecklesiologi if förhållande till praktiken med dubbelt medlemskap" in Alvarson, Jan-Åke, ed. *Församlingssyn i Pingströrelsen*, Forskningsrapport från Institutet för Pentekostala Studier 3, 29–41.

18. Seelsorger is a German term still used among English-speaking Lutherans for pastors who are known for their pastoral care and concern for their congregations. Roughly translated, it means a person who worries for

souls, and it pictures a man who has had more than his share of "dark nights of the soul" and spends long hours in prayer.

19. Bo Giertz, Herdabrev till Göteborgs stift (Stockholm: SKDB, 1949), 21–22.

Chapter 2

1. Kolb/Wengert, *The Augsburg Confession*, articles 4 and 5.

2. Martin Luther, *Against the Heavenly Prophets*, AE, Vol. 40, 213–214.

3. Magnus Hagevi, "Secularisation and Sacralisation at Three levels in Sweden from the Mid Twentieth Century" In kyrkohistorsk årskrift 111 (2011), 147–154.

4. Kolb/Wengert, *Smalcald Articles*, 322,3 and 323,10.

Chapter 3

1. Folke T. Olofsson, Svenka Kyrkan—Krisiti Kyrka? Vision och provocation in Imber, Rune, (ed) Talet om korset—Guds kraft, (Göteborg, Församlingsförlaget; 2005), 136.

2. Kilian McDonnel, *Christian Initiation and Baptism in the Holy Spirit: Evidence from the First Eight Centuries* (Collegeville, The Liturgical Press, 1994), 341–342.

3. Ibid, 144–145.

4. Peter Halldorf, *21 Kyrkofäder—historien om hur kristendomen formades*, (Örebro, Cordia; 2000), 39–40.

5. Jonathan Hill, *Den Kristna kyrkans historia*, (Örebro, Libris; 2013), 61.

6. Tomas Nygren, *Tillbaka till friheten—att tänka lutherskt idag* (Uppsala: EFS Budbäraren, 2017), 85.

7. Christian Braw, *Mystikens arv hos Martin Luther*, (Skellefteå, Artos; 1999), 84.

8. Martin Luther, LW 40:146, *Against the Heavenly Prophets in the Matter of Images and the Sacraments* (1525).

9. Regin Prenter, *Spiritus Creator: Luther's Concept of the Holy Spirit* (Philadelphia, Muhlenberg;1953), 254.

10. Braw, 13–17.

11. Martin Luther, "On the Councils and the Church," AE, Vol.41, 114.

12. Karl Witte, *Guds ord och löfte—dagliga betraktelser av Martin Luther* (Stockholm, SKDB; 1935).

13. Birgit Stolt, "Luther sälv-hjärtats och glädjens teolog," (Skellefteå, Artos; 2014).

14. Bernhard Lohse, *Martin Luther's Theology—Its Historical and Systematic Development* (Minneapolis, Fortress; 2011), 235.

15. Martin Luther, "Martin Luther's Commentary on Saint Paul's Epistle to the Galatians" (1535) Translated by Haroldo Camacho (Irvine, 1517 Publishing; 2018), 189–190.

16. Kolb/Wengert, *Large Catechism*, 436, 38; 439, 61–62.

17. William Barclay (1907-1978), Professor of Divinity and Biblical Criticism at the University of Glasgow.

18. Studiebibeln Nya Testament [Study Bible], Thoralf Gilbrand (ed) (Stockholm, Normans; 1983), 730.

Chapter 4

1. Martin Luther, *On Councils and the Church* AE, Vol 41, 148–150.

2. Kolb/Wengert, *Preface to the Augsburg Confession*, translation of the Latin text, paragraph 8, 33.

3. Cited in Car Axel Aurelius, *Hjärtpunkten—Evangeliets bruk som nyckeln till Augsburgska bekännelsen*, (Skellefteå, Artos, 1995), 43.

4. Aurelius, *Hjärtpunkten*, 41–45.

5. Bo Giertz, *Christ's Church*, location 2566–2572.

6. Ibid, loc. 2611.

7. Martin Luther, *The Freedom of a Christian*. AE Vol. 31, 345–346.

8. Martin Luther, *The Freedom of a Christian*. AE Vol. 31, 348.

9. Ibid, 351–2.

Chapter 5

1. Martin Luther "On the Councils and the Church" AE Vol. 41, 151.

2. Baptism, Eucharist and Ministry (2014), 21–22.

3. Kolb/Wengert, *The Small Catechism*, 359.

4. Martin Luther, "Letter to Two Pastors Concerning Rebaptism," http://www.lutheranpress.com/docs/DMBC-fulltext.pdf, March 22, 2018, 56.

5. Bengt Hägglund, *Trons Mönster* (Gothenburg Församlingsförlaget 2003), 95–96.

6. Kolb/Wengert, *Large Catechism*, 463, 53.

7. Philip Melanchthon, *Apology to the Augsburg Confession*, Concordia Triglotta (Milwaukee, Northwestern Publishing House, 1988), 199, 155.

8. Karl Barth, *Det Kristna Dopet*, (Örebro, Sweden: Westerbergs, 1949), 41.

9. Kolb/Wengert, *The Large Catechism, Baptism*, 461, 41.

Chapter 6

1. Martin Luther, "On Councils and the Church," 152.

2. Kolb/Wengert "*The Large Catechism, The Sacrament of the Altar*," 469, 23.

3. Herrens Måltid, Teologiska nätverket I Pingst, (Örebro, Sweden: Libris, 2009), 40–41.

4. Kolb/Wengert "*The Large Catechism. The Sacrament of the Altar*," 467, 1.

5. Ibid., 473–474.

6. Wilhelm Friedrich Besser, *Kristi lidandes och härlighets historia* (Stockholm: F&G Beijers, 1897), 55.

7. Kolb/Wengert, *The Large Catechism*, 467, 8–9.

8. Ibid., 469–470.

Chapter 7

1. Luther, "On the Councils and the Church," 153.

2. Christian Braw, *Mystikens arv hos Martin Luther* (Skellefteå, Sweden: Artos, 1998), 37.

3. Hans-Martin Barth, *The Theology of Martin Luther—A Critical Assessment*, (Minneapolis: Fortress Press, 2012), 7.

4. Translator's note. Seelsorger is a German word common even among American Lutherans to speak of a caretaker of souls, or a beloved pastor. I used it here in place of a Swedish word meaning roughly the same thing: själavådare.

5. Carl Axel Aurelius, *Hjärtpunkten*, 75.

6. Kolb/Wengert, *Augsburg Confession, Article 11*, 45.

7. Luther's house postil, the 19ᵗʰ Sunday after Trinity. [Huspostilla, http://logosmappen.net/uppbyggelse/luther/huspostillan/19_son_e_tref .htm] (10/04/2017).

8. Martin Luther, *House Postils, The first Sunday after Easter*.

9. Kolb/Wengert, *The Large Catechism, Baptism*, 465–66.

10. P.H.D. Lang (https://ctsfwmedia.s3.amazonaws.com/CTQ/CTQ %2056-4.pdf) Jan. 24, 2019, CTQ 56–4, PDF, 241.

11. Håkan Sunnliden, *Kyrkan—Guds Gåva* (Nya Hjälmseryd: Förlaget Åsnan, 1989), 77.

Chapter 8

1. Martin Luther, "On the Councils and the Church," 154.

2. Kolb/Wengert, *The Augsburg Confession, Art.* 5, 41.

3. Bo Giertz, *Christ's Church*, loc. 3888–3895.

4. Kolb/Wengert, *Apology to the Augsburg Confession Article* 13:7–9, 220.

5. Kolb/Wengert, *Apology of the Augsburg Confessions Article* 13:10–12, 220.

6. Kolb/Wengert, *Augsburg Confession Article* 14, 46.

7. Kolb/Wengert, *The Apology of the Augsburg Confession. Article* 14, 222–223.

Chapter 9

1. Martin Luther, "On the Councils and the Church," 164.

2. Kolb/Wengert, *The Large Catechism*, 386.

3. Ibid, 388.

4. Ibid, "For where one's head is right, one's whole life must also be right, and vice versa." Kolb/Wengert, 90.

5. Ibid, 389–90.

6. Ibid, Third Commandment, 399.

7. Yngve Brilioth, *Förord till Den svenska psalmboken* (1937)

8. Kolb/Wengert, *The Large Catechism, Baptism*, 457.

9. Gunnar Rosendal "Kyrklig förnyelse," (Helsingbord, Sweden: Gaudete, 2015), 128.

10. Berth Löndahl, "Ropet ur djupet och lovsången i höjden—högmässan och livsfrågorna i historia och nutid" i Svensk Pastoral tidskrift 57/3, 69.

11. Bo Giertz, Herdabrev till Göteborgs stift, (Stockholm, SKDB:1949), 53–54. This text can also be found in "Liturgy and Spiritual Awakening," the only chapter that has been translated from this book. It is held in the LCMS Liturgical Resources Archives Online.

Chapter 10

1. Martin Luther, "On the Councils and the Church," 164.

Postlude—The Church I See

1. John Lennon, "Imagine," track 1 on *Imagine*, Apple Records, 1971, LP record.